The SECOND SLICE

OVER 250 DELICIOUS, TIME-SAVING RECIPES
FOR GOLFERS AND PEOPLE ON THE GO

JACKIE EDDY

KEY PORTER BOOKS

Canadian Cataloguing in Publication Data
Eddy, Jackie, 1931–
   The second slice

Includes index.

ISBN 0-919493-60-2

1. Cookery. I. Title.

TX715.E33 1985   641.5   C85-098813-6

Key Porter Books Limited
70 The Esplanade
Toronto, Ontario
Canada M5E 1R2

85 86 87 88 1 2 3 4 5

Contents

Acknowledgements

To George, who never once complained about the increased food costs when I was conducting my final testing (well, maybe once or twice), to my eldest daughter Lynn, a wonderfully creative person, to my brother David for some very helpful editing, to Marion Parkins for support above and beyond the call of friendship and to my mother, a very special lady and an excellent cook, who seemed to have answers to all of my questions when I embarked on my cooking career. I would also like to thank the following friends for sharing their ideas with me.

Doreen Ayling, Joyce Butler, Lola Bradley, Eleanor Clark (my co-author of *The Absolute Beginner's Cookbook*), Barbara Chapman, Mary Collister, Jean Eddy, Myrtle French, Ehor Gauk, Patricia Gilley, Shirley Graham, Pal Hooper, Kay Ishi, Sheila Kelcher, Roberta Layton, Jane Liden, Betty Manning, Lorraine Little, Mary MacPhail, Sharon Marriott, Joan Rothschild, Mary Stenzel, Sheila Sterling, Terry Strain, Lisa Sorensen. Ed Needham's Listening Audience in Ottawa! A very special thanks to Patricia Hedge, my wine consultant!

Foreword

What is most important to me in food is *taste*. I want my family, my friends and my guests to feel that I have given them my best. And for most people, part of taste is appearance—really! I can *see* in my mind's eye most of the great meals I have eaten and I'll bet you can, too. So, my first two requirements for a recipe are that it delivers delicious *and* beautiful food — in a word, gourmet.

The golfer in me comes out in my next recipe requirements. Quick and easy, easy and quick! I want to spend the day parring the course (!) then serve luncheons and dinners that taste and look like they've demanded *hours*. My guess is that you have other things to do, too.

I guarantee you will find the recipes in this book delicious, lovely, quick and easy. Trust me. If I say to add a can of golden mushroom soup or even (beware, purists!) a spoonful of Bisto, trust me. Your guests will never know what noble shortcuts you've taken (until they ask for the recipe). If the list of ingredients calls for "one small can," don't worry about whether or not you have bought the *exact* small size I would have — the exact quantity is not specified because it's not important. So why worry about it? And when I suggest that you prepare a whole dish then stow it in the refrigerator ready to bake when you get home from the golf course, it's because it will turn out just as well as if you had prepared it the afternoon of your party — maybe better.

Make cooking a fairway wood to the green, a one putt for that birdie — bon appétit!

The First Hole: Appetizers

David's Cocktail Almonds   1 pound (450 g)

The just-right salty taste the soy sauce imparts to the skin of these toasty almonds will soon have you addicted.

1 pound unblanched almonds (450 g)
2 tablespoons soy sauce (30 mL)

Spread the almonds on a cookie sheet and bake in a preheated 350°F (180°C) oven for 20 to 25 minutes. The almonds should be toasty brown on the inside. Empty the almonds into a large bowl and immediately pour the soy sauce over them. Toss the almonds in the soy until they are well coated. (They will "hiss" and smell odd, but keep stirring!) Spread the nuts on a cookie sheet and let them dry for 1 to 2 hours.
    These tasty cocktail snacks can be stored in a jar for 1 to 2 months.

Artichoke Dip   About 2 cups (500 mL)

Here's a savory dip that can be made oven-ready in the morning or whipped up at a moment's notice.

10 ounce package frozen artichokes (275 g)
    OR
14 ounce can water-packed artichoke hearts (398 mL)
1 cup mayonnaise (250 mL)
3/4 cup grated Parmesan cheese (175 mL)

Cook the frozen artichokes in a small saucepan according to the directions on the package or drain the canned artichokes. Place the artichokes, mayonnaise and cheese in a blender or food processor and blend until smooth. Pour the dip into a small, oven-proof casserole dish and bake in a 350°F (180°C) oven for 10 to 12 minutes or until bubbly. This dip tends to separate if overbaked.
    Serve hot with bagels cut into bite-sized pieces for dippers.

Russian Blini

Have you ever heard of caviar with blini and wondered what the heck *blini* were? Well, they are little buckwheat pancakes on which you spread either whipped cream cheese or sour cream, then top with caviar.

Buckwheat flour is available at health food stores. Blini can be frozen, so all the work left for you at the last minute is to arrange the toppings for your lucky guests to spread.

Blini Batter
1 cup buckwheat flour (250 mL)
1 teaspoon baking powder (5 mL)
1 tablespoon sugar (15 mL)
1/8 teaspoon salt (0.5 mL)
1 egg, slightly beaten
3/4 cup lukewarm milk (175 mL)
1 teaspoon melted butter (5 mL)
2 tablespoons sour cream (30 mL)

Topping Suggestions
whipped cream cheese
sour cream
black caviar
red caviar
smoked salmon
finely shaved ham

To make the blini, sift the dry ingredients together three times. Combine the beaten egg, milk, butter and sour cream. Add the sifted dry ingredients to the combined liquids.

Pour about 1 teaspoon (5 mL) of batter for each pancake onto the griddle and fry, turning once when the edges begin to dry. Two-inch (5 cm) blini are about the right size. At this point, the blini may be cooled, then frozen.

To serve, arrange warm or room-temperature blini on a serving platter with a dish of whipped cream cheese or sour cream and the toppings of your choice.

Camembert Crisps

About 24 crisps

These are great with drinks before dinner or as an accompaniment to a thin soup.

4 ounces Camembert cheese (125 g)
1/2 cup butter (125 mL)
1/2 teaspoon Tabasco sauce (2 mL)
1/4 teaspoon seasoned salt (1 mL)
1 cup flour (250 mL)
2 tablespoons sesame seeds (30 mL)

Let the Camembert reach room temperature, then scrape the crust off with a knife. Place the cheese and butter in a food processor or mixer and blend well. Slowly blend in the Tabasco, seasoned salt and flour. With floured fingers, form a log about 14 by 1 1/4 inches (35 cm × 3 cm) on a piece of waxed paper. Wrap the log and refrigerate for a minimum of 3 hours.

Cut the chilled log into 1/8 to 1/4 inch (5 mm to 7 mm) slices and place the slices on a baking sheet. Sprinkle the cut surfaces with sesame seeds. Bake in a 400°F (200°C) oven for 10 to 12 minutes or until the edges are golden brown.

Serve warm.

Note: Camembert Crisps can be reheated in a 400°F (200°C) oven for 5 minutes to re-crisp.

Fried Camembert

1 small Camembert

If you are a Camembert fan, you will *love* this. If you are not a Camembert fan, you'll like it! The deliciously runny inside makes a wonderful contrast to the crisp outside, and the touch of sautéed green onion is pure heaven!

Look for a Camembert that is medium soft because a too-ripe cheese will melt while you are browning the crumbs.

7 ounce whole Camembert cheese (200 g)
1 egg, slightly beaten
1 cup fresh bread crumbs (250 mL)
4 tablespoons unsalted butter (60 mL)
   OR
2 tablespoons each of butter and oil (30 mL)
1/2 cup whole, chopped green onions (125 mL)
water biscuits or plain, unsalted crackers

Dip the whole, unskinned Camembert in the beaten egg, then into the bread crumbs. Make sure the whole cheese is well coated with crumbs. Set aside. (You can refrigerate the cheese at this point then cook it just before serving.)

Heat half of the unsalted butter (or half of the butter and oil) in a small skillet. Sauté the green onions until just soft. Set aside and keep warm.

Add the remaining butter (or butter and oil) to the skillet and fry the cheese round until brown on all sides. Use two wooden spoons to manipulate the cheese. Place the browned cheese on a small platter and surround it with small water biscuits or plain, unsalted crackers. Spoon the green onions on top of the cheese.

Serve hot.

Note: To serve Fried Camembert as a first course, cut the cheese into individual wedges. Increase the crumbs to 2 cups (500 mL) and use 2 eggs. Dip the wedges in the eggs, coat with crumbs, then deep fry until just golden brown — you don't want the cheese to melt.

Quick Baked Camembert

1 Camembert

I can't even think about this easy delicacy without having to swallow three or four times!

1 whole Camembert
chopped pecans
  OR
whole pine nuts
brown sugar

Have the cheese very cold. Cut the skin off the top of the Camembert, leaving a 1/4 inch (7 mm) border. Cover the top with nuts, pressing the nuts firmly into the cheese, then sprinkle with brown sugar. Place the Camembert on a *wooden board*—the cheese melts too rapidly if baked on a metal sheet. Bake in a very hot oven (about 475°F — 250°C) for about 10 minutes or until the sugar just starts to caramelize, but before the cheese starts to melt.

Serve with melba toast or water biscuits.

Caviar Spread

1 3/4 cups (425 mL)

I once placed this in front of my guests and went back to the kitchen to finalize the rest of the meal. Ten minutes later, I was ready for a well-deserved drink and a bit of Caviar Spread — it was gone! There were some guilty looking faces — particularly yours John L--g! When you taste this, you will understand John's problem.

Lumpfish caviar is fine for this dish. Your palate won't suffer, nor will your pocketbook.

8 ounces cream cheese (250 g)
1/2 cup sour cream (125 mL)
2 teaspoons grated, raw onion (10 mL)
2 teaspoons fresh lemon juice (10 mL)

3 1/2 ounces lumpfish caviar (92 g)

Combine all of the ingredients *except* the caviar and blend well. If the mixture seems to be too stiff, add an additional tablespoon (15 mL) of sour cream. Spoon the spread into a small glass bowl, cover and let sit for about 45 minutes in the refrigerator so the flavors have a chance to blend. The recipe can be prepared up to this point 2 to 3 days ahead.

At serving time, spread the caviar evenly on top of the cheese mixture and serve with toast rounds.

Beer Cheese

3 1/2 cups (875 mL)

You don't have to be a beer drinker to enjoy this tangy cheese spread— or the easy Beer Cheese Fondue in the Note below.

1 pound old Cheddar cheese, grated (450 g)
8 ounces cream cheese (250 g)
3/4 cup *flat* beer (175 mL)
2 tablespoons Worcestershire sauce (30 mL)
1 clove garlic, minced
1 teaspoon Tabasco sauce (5 mL)
1/4 teaspoon salt (1 mL)

Combine all the ingredients in a blender or food processor. Place the mixture in a crock or covered container and refrigerate overnight to allow the mixture to firm and the flavors to blend.

Beer Cheese keeps well in the refrigerator for several weeks.

Note: For a variation, heat Beer Cheese in a double boiler and use as a fondue with fresh French bread cubes for dunking.

Lynn's Liptauer Cheese Spread

1 1/2 cups (375 mL)

If you had a really hot game, hated to quit, so played a few extra holes, don't even bother reading the Note below. This spread is great to have on hand during the golfing season because it keeps so well in the refrigerator.

1/3 cup butter (75 mL)
8 ounces cream cheese (250 g)
2 teaspoons dry mustard (10 mL)
2 teaspoons water (10 mL)
1 tablespoon green onion, minced (15 mL)
4 anchovy fillets
1 1/2 tablespoons capers, minced (22 mL)
dash of caper juice
1 teaspoon dried parsley flakes (5 mL)
2 teaspoons paprika (10 mL)
salt to taste

Let the butter and cream cheese reach room temperature. In a small bowl, combine the mustard with the water and let stand for 5 minutes. Meanwhile, beat the butter and cream cheese until creamy. Add all the remaining ingredients. Refrigerate for about 45 minutes before serving so the flavors have time to blend. Serve in a small glass bowl surrounded by thin slices of dark bread.

This spread will keep for 2 to 3 weeks in the refrigerator. Do not freeze.

Note: If you really want to dress this up for a party (although, believe me, it doesn't need it), you can center the bowl of Liptauer on a large chilled platter and surround it with four "cups" made from Boston (Bibb) lettuce. Fill these cups with 4 tablespoons (60 mL) *each* of thinly sliced green onions, finely chopped radishes, chopped anchovy fillets and drained capers. Your guests spread some of the cheese on a piece of bread and sprinkle an assortment of accompaniments on top — like a mini salad!

Lise's Crab and Cheese Spread (or "Crab Pizza") 3 cups (750 mL)

You don't get to be a 3 handicap as Lise is by spending a lot of time in the kitchen, but she and her golf pro husband Muncie like to entertain, so having fool-proof and quick recipes on hand is a must.

16 ounces cream cheese, softened (450 g)
2 tablespoons Worcestershire sauce (30 mL)
2 tablespoons lemon juice (30 mL)
2 tablespoons mayonnaise (30 mL)
2 tablespoons grated onion (30 mL)
10 ounce bottle of chili sauce (285 mL)
   OR
seafood cocktail sauce
6 ounce can of crab, drained (175 g)

Combine the cheese, Worcestershire sauce, lemon juice, mayonnaise and grated onion. Mix well. Spread the mixture in a thin layer on a flat serving dish. Cover with plastic wrap and refrigerate until serving time.

At serving time pour the chili sauce (or seafood cocktail sauce) over the cheese mixture. Spread the crab on top of the sauce.

Serve with crackers.

Smoked Salmon, Brie and Pesto en Croûte

Serves 4

This creation was brought home to Edmonton via California in a dear friend's head. He tasted it, loved it and raved about it to me when he returned. I said come over *immediately* and we will try to re-create it. Our first attempt needed a little refining, but the second attempt was bang on!

4 inch round of Brie cheese (10 cm)
4 to 6 slices smoked salmon (enough to cover the top of the cheese)
1 to 2 tablespoons pesto sauce*, enough to spread over the salmon
   (15 mL to 30 mL)
14 ounce package frozen puff pastry (350 g)

Cut the Brie cheese in half to make 2 rounds. Top each half with slices of smoked salmon. Spread a thin layer of pesto sauce over the salmon. Let both cheese rounds sit in the freezer while you roll out the pastry, as you want the cheese just below the freezing stage.

Roll out 2 circles of pastry. Each should have a diameter that will allow you to encompass 1 cheese round. Immediately remove the cheese from the freezer and encompass each cheese round with the pastry. Seal the pastry well with water.

Place the wrapped cheese on a baking sheet, seam sides down, and bake in a preheated 375°F (190°C) oven for 20 to 25 minutes or until the pastry is golden brown.

Cut into wedges and serve immediately. As a luncheon dish, this is nice with a salad. It makes a wonderful appetizer all by itself.

* Pesto sauce is available in Italian markets.

Crab Tarts

2 to 3 dozen

Keep a package of frozen mini tart shells in the freezer and you can whistle up a very nice hors d'oeuvre in short order. What is even better is a package of Haust Snack Cups (red box, product of Holland)—they don't have to be prebaked, they just sit on the shelf waiting for an emergency.

5 to 7 ounce can of crab (142 g to 198 g)
1/2 cup mayonnaise (125 mL)
1 cup shredded Cheddar cheese (250 mL)
2 teaspoons dry sherry or lemon juice (10 mL)
1/4 teaspoon salt (1 mL)
1/4 teaspoon celery seed (1 mL)
pinch of white pepper

Combine all the ingredients. Spoon the mixture into miniature baked pastry shells or snack cups. Bake in a preheated 400°F (200°C) oven for 5 minutes — just long enough to heat the filling and melt the cheese.

Note: Shrimp, lobster or tuna may be substituted for the crab.

Smoked Salmon Mousse Crêpes Serves 6 to 8

1/3 pound chunk smoked salmon (175 g)
1/2 cup finely chopped onion (125 mL)
4 ounces cream cheese (125 g)
1/3 cup sour cream (75 mL)
1/2 teaspoon lemon juice (2 mL)
2 teaspoons capers (10 mL)
12 crêpes, 5 to 5 1/2 inches in diameter (12.5 cm to 14 cm)
fresh dill (garnish)

Place all the above ingredients in food processor and blend until smooth.
   Spread each crêpe with smoked salmon mousse and fold in quarters. Garnish with sprigs of fresh dill.
   Two crêpes per person makes a substantial first course.

Note: Now that you can buy ready-made crêpes, this makes a very easy first course. If you make your own crêpes, add 1 teaspoon (5 mL) dill to the batter.

Crab Wontons

4 to 5 dozen

Every time I have made this recipe, there have been fingers snatching the hot wontons as quickly as I fried them. Four to 5 dozen is a rough guess on quantity—I would have to get up in the middle of the night if I wanted an *exact* count!

These are really quite simple to make. Once you have the wrappers, the rest is easy. They freeze well and can be reheated in no time.

8 ounce package cream cheese (250 g)
6 ounce can of crab, drained (170 g)
2 tablespoons soft bread crumbs (30 mL)
1 egg yolk
2 pinches garlic powder
1/8 teaspoon Tabasco sauce (0.5 mL)
freshly ground black pepper to taste
1 package wonton wrappers
oil for deep frying

Have the cream cheese at room temperature and combine with the crab, bread crumbs, egg yolk, garlic powder, Tabasco and pepper. Mix well.

Put 1 teaspoon (5 mL) of filling just off-center on each 4 inch (10 cm) wonton wrapper square. Fold over at the center. Moisten edges with water and gently press together. Fold in half again lengthwise. Pull the two corners one over the other and press them together with a little water. A properly wrapped wonton resembles a nurse's cap!

Deep fry the wontons in oil (375°F – 190°C) for 2 to 3 minutes or until lightly browned and puffed.

The wontons can be frozen at this point. Freeze them on a cookie sheet, then "bag them" when they've frozen solid. To reheat, place frozen wontons on an ungreased cookie sheet and bake in a 400°F (200°C) oven for 7 to 10 minutes.

Serve hot with Plum Sauce for dipping — a commercial brand or your own. The following is very simple.

Plum Sauce
1/4 cup chili sauce (60 mL)
1/4 cup plum jelly or plum jam (60 mL)
3/4 scant teaspoon dry mustard (3 mL)
1/8 teaspoon Tabasco sauce (0.5 mL)

Put all the above ingredients in a small saucepan and heat until the jelly melts. Pour the sauce in a small dish and serve at room temperature.

This sauce can be made ahead. If you plan to serve all the wontons, double the sauce.

Fantastic During the Football or Après Ski Dip
Serves 12 to 14

Most golfers are great football fans and we are very big on après ski!

2 round loaves of pumpernickel bread
1/2 pound butter, room temperature (250 g)
16 ounces cream cheese (500 g)
1/3 cup minced onion (75 mL)
2 teaspoons Worcestershire sauce (10 mL)
1/4 teaspoon garlic powder (1 mL)
1/4 teaspoon paprika (1 mL)
1/8 teaspoon cayenne (0.5 mL)
about 1/3 cup beer (about 75 mL)

Hollow 1 of the pumpernickel loaves and tear the insides into bite-sized pieces for dipping. Tear or cut the other loaf into dipping pieces — dippers with a bit of crust are the best ones.

Whip together all the ingredients *except the beer*. Then whip in enough beer to make a good dipping consistency. You don't want the dip too runny.

At serving time, fill the hollowed loaf with dip and surround it with the torn bread dippers. I guarantee this will be consumed — shell and all.

Oriental Dip
1 1/3 cups (375 mL)

1 cup sour cream (250 mL)
1 teaspoon Chinese 5 spice powder (5 mL)
2 teaspoons soy sauce (10 mL)
1/4 cup chopped green onion (60 mL)
1 tablespoon mayonnaise (15 mL)

Blend all the ingredients and chill.

Use as a vegetable or shrimp dip. A great vegetable with this dip is jicama (pronounced "hicama").

Guacamole Party Dip

Serves 10 to 12

Slightly sensational, particularly if you serve it with your own taco chips, which are a snap to make, as you will see by the recipe that follows.

1st layer   Blend 8 ounces (250 g) cream cheese with 1 small clove of garlic, minced, and 1/4 cup (60 mL) sour cream

Spread this mixture on the bottom of a wide, shallow glass bowl, then add the remaining layers as follows:

2nd layer   1 large avocado, mashed (sprinkle lightly with lemon juice to prevent discoloration).

3rd layer   1 jalapeño pepper, chopped. This is a hot Mexican pepper. Use 2 peppers if you like it hot!

4th layer   1 tomato, finely chopped

5th layer   3 green onions, chopped

The dish can be assembled ahead of time up to this point. Cover and refrigerate until just before serving time.

At serving time pour one 8 ounce (250 mL) jar of Taco sauce over the top and sprinkle with grated Cheddar cheese and 4 slices cooked, crumbled bacon.

Serve with taco chips for dipping.

Taco Chips
corn or flour tortillas
3 to 4 cups oil for deep frying

If frozen, thaw the tortillas. Cut the tortillas in half, then cut each half into 2 or 3 wedge-shaped pieces, depending on the size you want. When the oil has reached about 375°F (190°C), add the tortilla pieces one by one. Do not crowd the pot. Cook until golden brown and crisp — about 1 minute. Fry in batches to the desired quantity. Cool on paper towels. If desired, salt the chips while they're cooling.

Chips can be made 1 day ahead.

Smoked Oyster Dip

1 cup (250 mL)

This is another of daughter Lynn's "finds." She came home from visiting her in-laws over the last holiday season and said she had disgraced herself by sitting next to the bowl of dip and eating practically the whole thing. She said, "I was out of control — I couldn't stop."

3 ounce can smoked oysters, drained (104 g)
4 ounces cream cheese (125 g)
1/4 cup sour cream (60 mL)
1 teaspoon Dijon mustard (5 mL)
2 drops Tabasco sauce

Put all the ingredients in a blender and blend until smooth — about 15 seconds.
  Nice with bread sticks or crackers.

Note: This dip can be made 3 to 4 days before serving time.

Hasty Hots

16 pieces

This recipe has been around for a long time and for very good reason — it is *so* easy. You always have the ingredients on hand and if you don't know about this quickie — you should.

4 green onions, finely chopped
1/2 cup grated Parmesan cheese (125 mL)
6 tablespoons mayonnaise (90 mL)
16 toast rounds

Combine the onions and cheese with enough mayonnaise to make a spread of a fairly firm consistency.
  Toast the toast rounds on one side under the broiler. Spread the cheese mixture on the *untoasted* sides of the bread. Place under the broiler until bubbly.

Liver Pâté

Serves 10 to 12

A very impressive first course can be made with this pâté. Use frozen puff pastry to encase the cooked and cooled pâté. Bake in a 425°F (220°C) oven until the pastry is cooked — about 20 to 25 minutes. Let cool. Bring the whole to the table. Slice moderately thin and serve on well-chilled plates. Pass Alison's Cumberland Sauce (page 50).

1/2 cup margarine (125 mL)
1 large onion, chopped
1 pound liver (450 g)
4 hard-boiled eggs
1/2 pound liverwurst (225 g)
1/2 teaspoon mace (2 mL)
1/4 teaspoon thyme (1 mL)
2 1/2 teaspoons brandy (12 mL)
salt and pepper to taste

Sauté the onion lightly in margarine. Put everything through a meat grinder — not a food processor or blender. Line a loaf pan (8 by 4 1/4 inches — 1.5 L) with foil. Put the mixture in the pan and cover with foil.

Bake in a 350°F (180°C) oven for 50 to 60 minutes or until firm in the center.

Serve with homemade melba toast (the recipe is in Ultra Easy — Appetizers).

Marinated Mushrooms on Rye Bread

10 to 12 pieces

These couldn't be easier — or more popular with mushroom lovers.

1/2 teaspoon garlic salt (2 mL)
1/4 cup vegetable oil (60 mL)
1/2 pound sliced raw mushrooms (225 g)
1/4 cup chopped green onions — mostly the white part, but include
  a little of the green (60 mL)
rye or whole wheat bread

Stir the garlic salt into the oil and pour it over the mushrooms. Add the chopped onions and stir. Let this sit in the refrigerator for 2 hours. Stir occasionally. Drain well and place on fingers of lightly buttered rye or whole wheat bread. (Make "fingers" by trimming the crusts from the bread and cutting the bread into thirds.)

Note: If I have fresh mushrooms left over in the refrigerator with no immediate use for them, I marinate them as above. Then they're ready to jazz up a slice of rye or a salad at a moment's notice.

Mushroom Pâté   Serves 8

I had almost forgotten about this appetizer until a friend called just recently to ask for the recipe.

2 tablespoons butter (30 mL)
1 medium onion
1/2 pound mushrooms (225 g)
1 1/2 tablespoons lemon juice (22 mL)
1 teaspoon Worcestershire sauce (5 mL)
1/2 teaspoon garlic salt (2 mL)
1/8 teaspoon pepper (0.5 mL)
1 tablespoon mayonnaise (15 mL)

Melt the butter in a skillet. Chop the onion in a food processor, taking care not to purée. Add it to the melted butter.

Chop the mushrooms in a food processor — again being careful not to purée. Add them to the onions along with the lemon juice, Worcestershire sauce, garlic salt and pepper.

Cook over medium heat, stirring frequently, until the juices evaporate and the mixture has the consistency of a pâté. Do not let the mixture brown. Remove from the heat and when cool, stir in the mayonnaise. Chill.

At serving time, empty into a small serving bowl and serve with crackers or toast fingers.

Note: This dish can be made a day or two before serving.

Sausage Balls

30 to 40 balls

3 cups Bisquick (750 mL)
1 pound sausage meat (450 g)
1 pound sharp Cheddar cheese, shredded (450 g)
1/2 cup water (125 mL)

Mix all the ingredients, kneading with your hands until they are well mixed. Form this mixture into balls about the size of walnuts. Place the balls on a cookie sheet and bake in a 350°F (180°C) oven for about 30 minutes.

Serve hot with toothpicks.

Sweet and Sour Sausage Balls

150 balls

Great for a large crowd. The balls can be made ahead and frozen. Simmer them in the sauce prior to serving.

4 pounds sausage meat (1.75 kg)
4 eggs
1 1/2 cups soft bread crumbs (375 mL)
3 teaspoons curry powder (15 mL)
1 teaspoon chili powder (5 mL)

Break up the sausage meat and add the eggs, bread crumbs, curry powder and chili powder. Mix well and shape into 3/4 inch (2 cm) balls. Brown over low heat on all sides, draining off the fat as it accumulates. Put the sausage balls on paper towels to drain. The balls can be frozen at this point.

Sauce
3 cups ketchup (750 mL)
1/2 cup white wine vinegar (125 mL)
1/2 cup soy sauce (125 mL)

Combine all the ingredients in a saucepan. Add the sausage balls and simmer for 30 minutes, stirring occasionally.

Serve with toothpicks (preferably from a chafing dish) and lots of napkins.

Note: If you freeze the balls, thaw them before adding them to the sauce.

Cheese Sticks

1 1/2 dozen pieces

Nice nibblers. Make a batch on a rainy day (or Men's Member-Guest Day!) and freeze it. These sticks are a nice accompaniment to salad and thin soups. I like to serve these on an hors d'oeuvre tray, standing upright in my favorite antique mug.

1/2 cup butter (125 mL)
1 cup flour (250 mL)
2 teaspoons dry mustard (10 mL)
1 teaspoon salt (5 mL)
1/8 teaspoon cayenne (0.5 mL)
1/4 cup water (60 mL)
1 1/2 cups old Cheddar cheese, grated (375 mL)
2 tablespoons grape nuts (30 mL)

Cream the butter. Sift the flour, mustard, salt and cayenne. Alternate working the sifted dry ingredients, water, cheese and grape nuts into the butter. Form the mixture into a ball, wrap in waxed paper and refrigerate for 1 to 2 hours.

Roll the chilled dough out on a well-floured surface and cut narrow strips. These may be twisted into spirals. Lay the spirals or flat strips on a cookie sheet and bake in a 300°F (150°C) oven for 12 to 15 minutes or until lightly browned.

Note: To re-crisp frozen Cheese Sticks, place in a 400°F (200°C) oven for 3 to 5 minutes. "Quickie" Cheese Sticks can be made by adding 1/2 pound (250 g) grated cheese to 2 Betty Crocker pie crust sticks. Increase oven temperature to 425°F (220°C) and bake for 8 minutes.

Whole Wheat Crackers   18 2-inch (5 cm) crackers

These make a nice "house gift" along with a small crock of Beer Cheese.

5 1/2 tablespoons oil (82 mL)
1/3 cup water (75 mL)
1 tablespoon brown sugar (15 mL)
1/2 teaspoon salt (2 mL)
1/2 cup quick cooking oats (125 mL)
3/4 cup wheat germ (175 mL)
3/4 cup whole wheat flour (175 mL)

Mix together the oil, water, brown sugar and salt and stir until the sugar and salt are dissolved. Stir in the oats, wheat germ and whole wheat flour. Form the dough into a ball.

Divide the ball in half and roll each half on ungreased smooth surface until very thin. If the dough starts to separate, just push it together with your fingers.

With a large knife, cut the dough into cracker-sized squares or rectangles. With a spatula, transfer these to a baking sheet and bake in a 350°F (180°C) oven for 15 minutes or until lightly browned.

ULTRA EASY — APPETIZERS

Savory cheese spreads are all the rage now. Make your own by whipping 4 ounces (125 mL) of cream cheese with 4 teaspoons (20 mL) of *creamy* horseradish, 1/4 teaspoon (1 mL) of hot dry mustard and 1/8 teaspoon (0.5 mL) of sugar. Serve your spread in a small glass bowl surrounded by crackers. When you get down to the "dregs," spread the last on Triscuits, top each cracker with an olive slice, broil until bubbly and serve hot.

Here's a good quickie for teenage parties and backyard barbecues. Dip *thin-sliced* bacon in Parmesan cheese and wrap it around a bread stick. Bake in a hot oven until the bacon is cooked.

Mix a little prepared mustard into mayonnaise for an easy vegetable dip. This is especially good with cherry tomatoes.

Keep a package of individual frozen tart shells in your freezer and fill them with your favorite quiche filling for unexpected guests.

Serve stuffed mushroom caps at your next large party — the easy way. Thaw a package of Stouffer's Spinach Soufflé, fill the caps and sprinkle them with Parmesan cheese. Stuff some more caps with Boursin cheese (these can be refrigerated overnight). Bake both kinds in a 350°F (180°C) oven for 10 minutes. A very attractive platter!

Pesto sauce (available at Italian markets) is another great mushroom filling. Use about 1 teaspoon (5 mL) of sauce for each cap. Bake in a 350°F (180°C) oven for about 8 minutes.

Don't throw dill pickle juice away! Boil carrot sticks in the juice until they are just crisp-tender. Chill, then serve garnished with fresh dill.

Unsliced hot dog buns and bagels, cut in rounds, are a nice size for canapés.

To make melba toast, roll slices of bread with a rolling pin until they are very thin. Butter the slices on both sides and bake them in a moderate oven until golden brown.

The Second Hole: Soups

Bean and Vegetable Soup Serves 10

Everyone loves a bowl of hearty soup (*not* with a seven course dinner, please). Serving a tureen of steaming, flavorful soup has become a popular buffet feature for informal entertaining. Borrow an additional tureen from a friend and offer a choice—this soup at one end, the Corn Chowder at the other end. Some Quick Whole Wheat Bread (page 151) and good aged Cheddar in the center make a lovely main course. Have some fresh fruit, walnut or peach flavored cream cheese (my brother Donald calls these "sissy" cheese) and gooey squares with a pot of good coffee and you have a fairly inexpensive party.

2 large onions, chopped
1 tablespoon each of butter and oil (15 mL)
2 stalks celery, diced
1 small green pepper, diced
2 large carrots, diced
2 14-ounce cans stewed tomatoes, cut up (2 398 mL)
4 cups beef stock or chicken stock (1 L)
2 14-ounce cans mild chili con carne, with beans (2 398 mL)
1/2 teaspoon sugar (2 mL)
pinch of ground cloves
pinch of garlic powder
salt and pepper to taste

Sauté the onions in the oil and butter until soft. Add the celery and green pepper and continue to sauté for about 5 minutes, stirring fairly frequently. Add all the other ingredients and simmer, covered, for about 30 minutes. Stir occasionally.

Note: This soup is very much like minestrone. Add a little broken, uncooked spaghetti or macaroni and you could almost call it minestrone!

Mary's Carrot and Orange Soup   Serves 8

When someone is describing a particular dish and she rolls her eyes, I am hooked and can't wait to try it. Mary was no sooner out the door before I was on my way to the grocery store for the carrots and orange juice! For an interesting presentation, see the Note below.

2 cups sliced carrots (500 mL)
1/4 cup butter (60 mL)
1/2 cup chopped onion (125 mL)
5 cups chicken broth (1.25 L)
3 tablespoons flour (45 mL)
6 ounces thawed, frozen orange juice *concentrate* (175 mL)
1/2 teaspoon salt (2 mL)
1/8 teaspoon pepper (0.5 mL)
1 cup cereal cream (250 mL)
1 teaspoon chopped green onion (5 mL)
chopped parsley (garnish)

Cook the carrots in a small amount of water, drain and set aside.

Melt 2 tablespoons (30 mL) of the butter in a small frying pan and sauté the onions for 3 to 4 minutes. Purée the onions with 2 cups (500 mL) of the chicken broth and the carrots in a blender or food processor.

Melt the remaining 2 tablespoons (30 mL) of butter in a large saucepan, stir in the flour and cook until well blended. Slowly add the remaining 3 cups (750 mL) of chicken broth and cook until slightly thickened. Add the orange juice concentrate, salt, pepper, cream, onion and carrot mixture and green onion. Stir until well blended but do not allow to boil.

Serve hot in the winter, cold in the summer. Garnish with chopped parsley.

Note: If you plan to serve this cold, orange cups make perfect little containers. Cut off the top third of oranges and scoop the pulp out with a grapefruit knife. The fruit can be saved for a fruit salad the following day. A few sections may be saved for a garnish.

Champagne and Camembert Soup

Serves 4 to 6

There is a great camaraderie among golfers — instant friends! This recipe came to me as a result of the Commonwealth Golf Tournament recently held in Alberta. The Rothschilds were a delightful extension of the British team. It didn't take long to establish the fact that we all were interested in good food. This soup was the result. Keep it in mind for your next gourmet dinner. Thank you Joan!

1/2 cup butter (125 mL)
2 tablespoons flour (30 mL)
1 cup chicken stock (250 mL)
2/3 cup milk (150 mL)
1 cup cereal cream (250 mL)
12 3/4 ounces Camembert (405 g)
5 ounces Spanish-type champagne or dry sparkling white wine (150 mL)
salt and pepper
chopped parsley (garnish)

Melt 2 tablespoons (30 mL) of the butter and blend in the flour. Slowly pour in the stock and stir with a wire whisk until boiling. Simmer for 2 to 3 minutes or until it starts to thicken. Slowly add the milk and cream and return to just below the boiling point.

Remove the mixture from the heat and stir in the rest of the butter until melted and absorbed. Place back on low heat and cut in the Camembert in very small pieces, including the rind. Stir until the cheese has melted completely.

Press the soup through a sieve into another saucepan. Heat but *do not allow to boil*. Stir in the champagne. Season with salt and pepper.

Serve in small portions, garnished with chopped parsley.

Note: This soup can be prepared in advance *up to* the addition of the champagne. Just before serving, reheat but *do not boil* the soup, then stir in the champagne.

Bombay Consommé with Cheese Balls

Serves 6

If you are planning a multi-course dinner, this is an excellent choice for the soup course.

2 10-ounce cans consommé (2 284 mL)
10 ounces apple juice (284 mL)
2/3 teaspoon curry powder (2.5 mL)
1/4 cup dry sherry (60 mL)

Combine the consommé, apple juice and curry. Bring to a simmer and add the cheese balls. Simmer for 3 to 5 minutes. Remove from the heat and stir in the sherry.

Cheese Balls   **Approximately 24 balls**

1 1/2 cups grated Gouda cheese (375 mL)
2 tablespoons grated Parmesan cheese (30 mL)
1 egg
1 tablespoon melted butter (15 mL)
1 tablespoon bread crumbs (15 mL)
1 teaspoon chopped parsley (5 mL)
1/2 teaspoon paprika (2 mL)
no salt

Combine all the ingredients. Mix well and place in the refrigerator for about 10 minutes for easier handling. Form into small balls (about 1/2 inch — 1.5 cm in diameter) and simmer in the soup for 3 to 5 minutes just before serving.

Note: Most of the work for this soup can be done in advance — simply wait to add the sherry and the cheese balls just before serving time.

Two Minute Chinese Soup

Serves 4

I don't often serve a Chinese dinner. I am not a last minute person and so much of Chinese cooking is last minute. When I do — I start with this almost instant soup and instant success!

2 10-ounce cans of chicken broth, undiluted (2 284 mL)
2 cans of water
1 package Ichiban soup (or any of the instant noodles with flavored soup stock)
1/4 pound sliced fresh shrimp or tiny whole shrimp (125 g)
1 small can sliced water chestnuts
a few sliced fresh mushrooms
1 cup frozen peas (250 mL)

Bring the broth and water to a boil. Add all the remaining ingredients — dried noodles, shrimp, water chestnuts, mushrooms and peas — *except* the soup flavor packet. Simmer for 2 minutes only. Do not overcook. Stir in the flavor packet, which comes with the dried noodles.

Corn Chowder

Serves 8

Every so often I crave a steaming bowl of Corn Chowder. If the craving is intense and I want to hurry the soup along I substitute canned potato soup for the cubed and cooked potatoes.

6 slices bacon
1/2 cup chopped onion (125 mL)
1/2 green pepper, chopped
2 cups milk (500 mL)
1 cup light cream (250 mL)
1 cup shredded carrot (250 mL)
1 teaspoon salt (5 mL)
1/8 teaspoon pepper (0.5 mL)
1 1/2 cups potatoes, cubed and cooked (375 mL)
1 tablespoon butter (15 mL)
2 14-ounce cans cream-style corn (2 398 mL)

Fry the bacon, remove and set aside. Remove all but 2 tablespoons (30 mL) bacon fat from pan. Add the onion and green pepper and sauté until soft. Crumble the bacon. Add the remaining ingredients, including the crumbled bacon. Simmer for 2 minutes.

Cream of Fiddlehead Soup

Serves 4

Fresh fiddleheads are available only in early spring and like any other vegetable the fresh is always better than the frozen. I wouldn't use fresh fiddleheads for soup; however, serving something a little different is always fun and the frozen fiddleheads make an interesting soup you might want to consider for your next dinner party.

1 medium leek, chopped (white part only)
2 tablespoons butter (30 mL)
1 package McCain's frozen fiddleheads
1 medium potato, diced
3 cups of your best chicken stock (or canned, undiluted chicken stock) (750 mL)
pinch of thyme
salt and pepper to taste
1 cup cereal cream (250 mL)

Sauté the leek in butter until tender but not browned. Add the fiddleheads, cover and let steam over low heat for 10 to 15 minutes. Add the potato, chicken broth and seasonings. Simmer for 15 minutes or until the potato is tender. Put the mixture through a blender or food processor. Return to pot, correct seasoning and stir in the cream. Do not allow to boil once the cream has been added.

Serve hot garnished with a few croutons or float a slice of raw mushroom on top.

Note: This soup can be reheated but do not allow it to come to a boil after the cream has been added.

Patricia's Lemon Velvet Soup   Serves 4 to 6

Definitely company fare!

1 tablespoon cornstarch (15 mL)
2 cups chicken bouillon (500 mL)
1 cup light cream (250 mL)
3 egg yolks at room temperature
1/2 cup fresh lemon juice (125 mL)
pinch of cayenne
very thin slices of fresh lemon (garnish)
chopped parsley (garnish)

Dissolve the cornstarch in 1 tablespoon (15 mL) of the chicken bouillon. In a saucepan combine the remaining bouillon and the cream. Stir in the cornstarch mixture. Cook the soup over low heat until it starts to thicken. Do not let it boil or it will curdle.

Beat the egg yolks lightly and beat a bit of the hot soup into eggs to warm them slightly, stirring constantly. Add the yolks, lemon juice and cayenne to the hot soup while continuing to stir. Remove from the heat and chill overnight.

Serve in chilled soup bowls and garnish with a very thin slice of lemon and a bit of chopped parsley.

"Irish" Onion Soup   Serves 4 to 6

If you think waistlines will allow, top each serving with tiny sautéed cubes of salt pork — well rendered.

4 tablespoons butter (60 mL)
3 1/2 cups sliced onion (875 mL)
3/4 cup chopped green onion (175 mL)
1 clove garlic, minced
2 tablespoons flour (30 mL)
2 10-ounce cans chicken broth (2 284 mL)
1 soup can of water
1/2 teaspoon salt (2 mL)
1/8 teaspoon white pepper (0.5 mL)
1/2 cup cereal cream (125 mL)
1 tablespoon chopped parsley (15 mL)
pinch of nutmeg

In a heavy saucepan melt the butter, then add the onions, green onions and garlic. Cook, stirring occasionally, for about 15 minutes. You want the vegetables golden brown but not burned. Stir in the flour. Gradually add the chicken broth and water and simmer, covered, for 30 minutes.

Purée the soup in a blender or food processor. Return to saucepan and add the salt, pepper, cereal cream, parsley and nutmeg. Heat but do not allow to boil.

Serve at once.

Spinach, Leek and Potato Soup   Serves 8

This soup may be made the day before and reheated — it is *the* favorite soup of my daughter Louise and any leftovers are always hers!

6 medium leeks, sliced (white part only)
2 tablespoons butter (30 mL)
4 cups chicken stock (1 L)
2 10-ounce packages frozen spinach (2 275 g)
3 medium potatoes, peeled and sliced
2 cups light cream (500 mL)
salt and pepper to taste
pinch of nutmeg

Sauté the leeks in the butter until limp, but not brown. Place them in a saucepan with the chicken stock, spinach and potatoes. Simmer all together until the potatoes are cooked.

Put the soup in a blender and blend until smooth. Return to the saucepan and add cream, salt, pepper and nutmeg. Heat but do not allow to boil.

Wild Rice and Mushroom Soup   Serves 6

If you have access to wild mushrooms — this is transformed from a great soup into a fantastic soup!

4 tablespoons butter (60 mL)
1/4 cup finely chopped onion (60 mL)
1/4 cup finely chopped celery (60 mL)
1/2 pound fresh mushrooms, thinly sliced (225 g)
1/4 cup flour (60 mL)
4 cups chicken bouillon (1 L)
1/2 teaspoon salt (2 mL)
1 1/2 cups cooked wild rice (375 mL)
1 cup cereal cream (250 mL)
2 tablespoons dry sherry (30 mL)
chopped fresh parsley (garnish)

Melt the butter and sauté the onions, celery and mushrooms until tender. Sprinkle flour over the top and blend in. Gradually add the chicken bouillon and salt, stirring constantly until thickened, about 5 minutes. Cover and simmer an additional 5 minutes. Stir in the rice and simmer for 2 to 3 minutes.

Stir in the cream and sherry and cook until well heated but do not allow to boil. Garnish with chopped fresh parsley.

Note: This soup can be made ahead of time up to the addition of the cream and sherry. Just before serving, reheat, then add the cream and sherry and bring to a serving temperature (do not allow to boil).

Zucchini Soup

Serves 4

I am always looking for ways to use zucchini once our garden starts producing . . . and producing and producing! This makes a delicious cold summer soup. It is also good hot. Try it both ways and decide which *you* like best.

3 to 4 medium zucchini, cubed and unskinned
salt
1 onion, finely minced
1 clove garlic, finely minced
4 tablespoons butter or margarine (60 mL)
2 10-ounce cans chicken broth (undiluted) (2 284 mL)
1/8 teaspoon white pepper (0.5 mL)
2 pinches nutmeg
1/2 cup cereal cream (125 mL)
chopped fresh parsley, chives or thinly sliced mushrooms (garnish)

Place the cubed zucchini in colander and sprinkle it with salt. Allow to drain for about 30 minutes.

In a large soup pot or Dutch oven, sauté the onions and garlic in the butter until the onions are soft and slightly golden. Dry the zucchini on paper towels and add it to the pot. Cook over low heat for about 5 minutes, stirring frequently. Add the chicken broth and simmer for about 15 minutes.

Purée the soup in a blender or food processor. Return it to the pot and add the pepper, nutmeg and cream. Test for salt. It should be salty enough with the salt clinging to the cubed zucchini in the draining process.

Garnish with chopped fresh parsley, chives or a few very thin slices of raw mushroom.

Note: The thickness can be adjusted with more or less zucchini — the more, the thicker. The really large homegrown zucchini are not really suitable as they are very watery.

ULTRA EASY — SOUPS

For an almost-instant soup, put 1 1/2 tablespoons (22 mL) of cooked and crumbled bacon in the bottom of a soup bowl. Cover the bacon with heated but *not* boiled V-8 juice and sprinkle Parmesan cheese on top.

For a delicious Clam Vichyssoise, add minced clams and a little heavy cream to the best available canned vichyssoise.

For a real gourmet touch, top individual servings of vichyssoise with a bit of *red* caviar (the black is unsightly).

Celery leaves, dried in a very slow oven (250°F — 130°C) are a wonderful flavoring for soups and stews. Crumble the dry leaves when they're cool and store them in a jar.

Combine a 10 ounce (284 mL) can of condensed tomato soup with a 10 ounce (284 mL) can of condensed pea soup, 1 cup (250 mL) of milk, 1 cup (250 mL) of water and a dash of curry powder and you can serve a soup that is not only delicious, but that nobody will ever guess came right out of a can!

For a light accompaniment to a soup course, spread a mixture of butter and soy sauce on toast, sprinkle generously with sesame seeds and place in a hot oven until toasted. Cut into fingers and serve hot.

Another light accompaniment to a soup course can be made with wonton wrappers. Brush a little melted butter on each uncooked wrapper, lightly sprinkle the wrappers with curry powder and bake them in a 375°F (190°C) oven for 5 to 6 minutes. (These keep well and also make a nice cocktail snack.)

Quick dumplings can be made for a hearty soup by combining 1 beaten egg, 1/4 cup (60 mL) of milk and 1 cup (250 mL) of Bisquick. Simmer the dumplings in hot soup for 15 to 20 minutes.

Always sauté vegetables before adding them to soups. This allows the vegetables to "sweat" and to absorb the butter flavor.

The Third Hole: Salads

Bread Bowl
(container for salads)
Holds salad for 6

This is a fun way to serve a salad. Once the salad has been served, the bowl is eaten. Just enough of the dressing penetrates to make the bread wonderfully delicious.

1 loaf of Italian bread, approximately 12 inches (30 cm) in diameter
2 eggs
2 tablespoons milk (30 mL)

Use a bread knife to cut the top third from a large Italian loaf. Cut around the perimeter of the loaf, leaving a 3/4 inch (2 cm) border of crust, and hollow out the center. Beat the eggs with the milk to make a glaze and brush it over the inside of the loaf. Wrap foil around the *outside* of the loaf and place it on a baking sheet. Bake in a preheated 350°F (180°C) oven for 20 to 25 minutes. Set aside to cool.

Note: My daughter Lynn took this a step further—rather than painting the inside, she painted the baked, cooled bowl on the *outside* with varithane and allowed it to dry. She now stores this "conversation piece container" so that it's always on hand for entertaining. Make sure you line the inside well with the plastic wrap, for you don't want any of the food to come in contact with the varnish finish. (Lynn suggests that you cut a hole in the loaf the size of a bread and butter plate if you plan to make a permanent bread bowl.)

Avocado Salad in Edible Bowls   Serves 6

This isn't nearly as hard as it looks and it's guaranteed to impress! Most of the work can be done the day before your party.

6 corn or flour tortillas
oil for deep frying (about 1 1/2 inches — 4 cm deep)
1 head Boston or Bibb lettuce
2 medium tomatoes
1 medium avocado
1/2 medium green pepper, diced
2 green onions, sliced
4 slices bacon, cooked and crumbled
   OR
1/2 cup Cheddar cheese, grated (125 mL)

If the tortillas are frozen, let them thaw. To make the salad bowls, heat the oil in a saucepan to a depth of about 1 1/2 inches (4 cm). Place a tortilla in the hot oil and *immediately* place the bowl of a large non-plastic soup ladle in the center of the tortilla. Hold the ladle in place until the tortilla is cooked and will maintain the shape. This takes only a minute or two. Remove the "tortilla bowl" to a paper towel to cool.

To make the salad, tear the lettuce into salad-sized pieces and set aside in a large bowl. Dice the tomatoes and avocado; put these in a small bowl and pour half the salad dressing over them (see recipe below). Just before serving, combine the lettuce, avocado, tomatoes and green pepper and toss in the remaining dressing. Arrange the salad mixture in the tortilla bowls and top each with the sliced green onions and either crumbled bacon or grated Cheddar cheese.

Salad Dressing   About 1/2 cup (125 mL)
1/3 cup salad oil (75 mL)
1 1/2 tablespoons cider vinegar (22 mL)
1 teaspoon lemon juice (5 mL)
3/4 teaspoon chili powder (3 mL)
1/4 teaspoon salt (1 mL)
1/8 teaspoon freshly ground black pepper (0.5 mL)
1/2 teaspoon sugar (2 mL)

Combine all the ingredients in a small jar and shake them until well blended. This dressing can be made a day or two ahead of time.

Raw Cauliflower Salad

Serves 6

Try serving a cauliflower salad to add variety to your meals. People love the crunchy texture of cauliflower, particularly young people. I have a daughter who won't touch cooked cauliflower, yet loves this salad. It is difficult to give exact amounts as heads of cauliflower vary so much in size, but for a general rule of thumb, 1 medium head will serve 6.

1 medium head raw cauliflower
1/2 to 1 cup Miracle Whip (125 mL to 250 mL)
1/4 cup Parmesan cheese (60 mL)
1/4 cup bacon chips (60 mL)

Soak the cauliflower in cold salted water for 30 minutes. Drain and break into tiny flowerets. Stir in enough Miracle Whip to moisten. Just before serving, sprinkle with Parmesan cheese and bacon chips. Toss and serve.

Wilted Cucumber Salad

Serves 10 to 12

A refreshing summer salad — good with hot or cold meats. Especially good with salmon.

3 cucumbers
1 teaspoon salt (5 mL)
1 small onion, grated
3/4 cup sour cream (175 mL)
1/2 cup sugar (125 mL)
4 tablespoons apple cider vinegar (60 mL)
1/4 teaspoon white pepper (1 mL)

Peel the cucumbers and slice thinly. Mix with the salt and grated onion Place a heavy weight on the cucumber and onion mixture and let sit overnight. On the next day drain well.

Make a sauce by combining the sour cream, sugar, vinegar and pepper. Mix the sauce with the cucumbers and chill well.

Joy's Cheese and Lettuce Salad Serves 8 to 10

You can make most of this the night before or in the morning as my busy schoolteacher friend does.

1/2 pound Swiss Gruyère cheese, shredded (250 g)
1 cup sliced green onion (250 mL)
1 cup diced celery (250 mL)
1 cup sliced olives (250 mL)
1 cup diced green pepper (250 mL)
1/2 cup olive oil (125 mL)
2 1/2 tablespoons red wine vinegar (37 mL)
1 tablespoon prepared mustard (15 mL)
1/2 teaspoon salt (2 mL)
freshly ground pepper to taste
4 cups shredded lettuce (1 L)

Combine cheese, onions, celery, olives and green pepper in a large bowl. Beat oil, vinegar, mustard, salt and pepper in small bowl. Pour the dressing over the cheese mixture. Toss to blend. Let stand for a minimum of 30 minutes (or overnight). Just before serving toss with shredded lettuce.

Grape Salad   Serves 6 to 8

This is probably the best of the sour cream-marshmallow type fruit salads, which can be made the day before serving and are extremely popular.

1 cup sour cream (250 mL)
1 cup green seedless grapes, halved (250 mL)
1 cup black grapes, seeded and halved (250 mL)
1 cup red grapes, seedless or seeded and halved (250 mL)
1 cup pineapple tidbits, drained (250 mL)
1 cup miniature marshmallows (250 mL)

Combine all the ingredients and let sit overnight.

Large Chicken Salad

Serves 16

If you have some of "the girls" back for lunch after a golf game, this is perfect, because it can be made the night before. Take the buns and dessert out of the freezer before you leave for the golf course. For smaller chicken salads (made with leftover chicken) see the Leftovers section. For the best way to cook the chicken breasts, see the Note below.

2 1/2 cups mayonnaise (625 mL)
2 1/2 teaspoons curry powder (12 mL)
2 1/2 teaspoons soy sauce (12 mL)
6 to 8 whole chicken breasts, cooked and coarsely cubed
20 ounce can water chestnuts, sliced (568 mL)
2 cups seedless green grapes (500 mL)
2 cups sliced celery (500 mL)
2 to 3 cups toasted, slivered almonds (500 mL to 750 mL)
19 ounce can pineapple chunks, drained (550 mL)
2 10-ounce cans mandarin oranges, drained (2 284 mL)

Mix the mayonnaise with the curry powder and soya sauce. Fold in all the remaining ingredients. Refrigerate for several hours or overnight.
Serve on lettuce leaves with warm buns.

Note: Best-ever Steamed Chicken Method
The best way to cook chicken for a salad (or for plain sliced cold chicken) is the following "steamed" method. The Chinese have been doing this for years. The chicken is actually steeped rather than cooked, which produces moist, white chicken pieces.

Place the chicken breasts in a large pot, just big enough to hold them. Add enough water to cover the chicken up to 1/2 inch (1.5 cm) over the top. Remove the chicken. Add 1 or 2 green onions to the water and bring to a boil. Lower the chicken carefully back into the pot. When the water returns to a boil, boil for 3 minutes. Cover tightly, *turn heat off*, then let sit for a minimum of 3 hours. It can sit for as long as 6 hours, but then it should be refrigerated.

Strain the stock and save it for soups, sauces and gravies.

Crab Louis   Serves 6

If you feel your budget being squeezed when you check the price of crab you can substitute cooked halibut, which tastes much like crab, or use a combination of both.

3 cups fresh crabmeat (750 mL)
3 hard-cooked eggs, chopped or cut in wedges
2 tomatoes, cut in wedges
1 small head of lettuce, shredded

Arrange the crabmeat on a bed of shredded lettuce. Pour the Louis Dressing over this. Arrange the tomatoes and hard-cooked eggs on top of or around the crab.

Louis Dressing
1 cup mayonnaise (250 mL)
1/4 cup chili sauce (60 mL)
1/4 cup cream (60 mL)
1/4 cup chopped green onion (60 mL)
1/4 cup chopped green pepper (60 mL)
2 tablespoons chopped green olives (30 mL)
1/2 teaspoon salt (2 mL)
1 teaspoon horseradish (5 mL)
lemon juice to taste

Combine all the above ingredients and shake well.

Greek Salad   Serves 8 to 10

1 clove garlic
2 large heads romaine lettuce, torn in bite-sized pieces
4 tomatoes, cut in wedges
2 cucumbers, peeled and thinly sliced
2 onions, very thinly sliced (preferably red)
2 ounce can anchovies, drained, rinsed and patted dry (50 g)
1/4 cup chopped fresh parsley (60 mL)
1 cup feta cheese, drained and crumbled* (250 mL)
1 cup Greek black olives (250 mL)

Rub a large wooden salad bowl with the clove of garlic. Discard the garlic. Arrange the lettuce attractively with the tomatoes, cucumbers, onions, anchovies and parsley. Sprinkle the feta cheese and Greek olives on top. Make sure your salad ingredients are well chilled.

Just before serving, pour the following dressing over the salad.

Vinaigrette Dressing
3/4 cup olive oil (no substitutes) (175 mL)
1/4 cup red wine vinegar (60 mL)
1 teaspoon Dijon mustard (5 mL)
3/4 teaspoon salt (3 mL)
1/8 teaspoon freshly ground black pepper (0.5 mL)
1 teaspoon oregano (5 mL)

Combine all the ingredients in a jar and shake until blended. This dressing will keep well in the refrigerator.

* If you soak the feta cheese in milk for 2 hours before serving, the flavor improves.

Spinach Salad
Serves 4

1/2 pound fresh spinach (225 g)
1/4 cup salad oil (60 mL)
1 tablespoon red wine vinegar (15 mL)
1 teaspoon lemon juice (5 mL)
1/8 teaspoon salt (0.5 mL)
freshly ground pepper to taste
1/8 teaspoon garlic powder (0.5 mL)
1 tablespoon Parmesan cheese, grated (15 mL)
4 slices crisp bacon, crumbled
1 hard-cooked egg, chopped (optional)

Trim off and discard any tough stems or bruised spinach leaves. Wash well in cold water. Shake off any excess water or pat with paper towels. Tear the leaves into bite-sized pieces.

Combine the oil, vinegar, lemon juice, salt, pepper, garlic powder and Parmesan cheese. Blend well.

When ready to serve, toss the spinach with the dressing and sprinkle with the crumbled bacon. If you're adding chopped egg, sprinkle it on top with the bacon.

Note: Sunshine Salad Dressing (see page 47) is excellent on spinach.

Overnight Layered Salad

Serves 8

The secret to keeping this salad fresh is the "sealing off" of the salad ingredients by the salad dressing — so don't alter the dressing. A too-runny dressing will run down the sides of the bowl into the lettuce and create a rather soggy mess in the bottom.

1 head iceberg lettuce, coarsely shredded
1/2 cup chopped green pepper (125 mL)
1/2 cup chopped green onion (125 mL)
1/2 cup chopped celery (125 mL)
10 ounce package frozen tiny peas (275 g)

Put the above ingredients in salad bowl in layers in the order given.

Dressing
1 cup mayonnaise (250 mL)
1 cup sour cream (250 mL)
2 tablespoons sugar (30 mL)

Mix the mayonnaise, sour cream and sugar together well and spoon carefully over the top layer in the bowl, which will be the frozen peas. Cover and place in the refrigerator overnight.

Have ready
1 cup shredded Cheddar cheese (250 mL)
8 slices crisp bacon, crumbled

Sprinkle the cheese and bacon over the top of salad just before serving. *Do not toss.*

Mexican Salad

Serves 10 to 12

This is a very recent find and I "found" it in the middle of the supermarket when I ran into my aerobics teacher, who is also a fellow golfer. There hasn't been a spoonful left any time I have served it. It is great for backyard barbecues or to take along for pot luck suppers. The proportions are flexible. I have given the recipe for 12 but you can cut it in half, double or triple it easily.

1 head iceberg lettuce, shredded
1 small red cabbage, shredded
1 red onion (or any mild onion), thinly sliced
14 ounce can garbanzo or kidney beans* (398 mL)
1 cup shredded Monterey Jack cheese (250 mL)
1 cup shredded Cheddar cheese (250 mL)
1 1/2 teaspoons chili powder (7 mL)
8 ounce bottle Catalina dressing (250 mL)
1 small package tortilla chips, broken

Put all ingredients in large salad bowl in layers as named *except* the chili powder, dressing and chips. Add the chili powder to the dressing. At serving time, add the chips and dressing to the salad ingredients. Toss and serve.

* If you double the recipe, add one can of each.

Mediterranean Salad Serves 10 to 12

I was going to call this "kitchen shelf salad" but I thought it sounded boring, which this salad is not. It has several good features which include having most of the ingredients always on hand for unexpected guests and being able to make most of it ahead of time — and great taste!

14 ounce can ripe olives (398 mL)
6 1/2 ounce jar marinated artichoke hearts (184 mL)
10 ounce can button mushrooms (284 mL)
14 ounce can garbanzo beans (398 mL)
1 1/2 cups sliced celery, including some of the tops (375 mL)
1/2 cup chopped green onion (125 mL)
14 ounce can whole baby beets (398 mL)
Italian dressing or Mustard Vinaigrette Dressing (page 46)
Optional:
1 cup diced mozzarella cheese (250 mL)
2 ounce can anchovies, drained and cut up (50 g)

Make sure all of the canned vegetables are *well drained*. Marinate all of the canned vegetables except the beets (the color will run) in your favorite Italian dressing or the Mustard Vinaigrette Dressing on page 46 and chill for at least 1 hour. This can be done in the morning or the night before. At serving time, toss with remaining ingredients.

Pasta Salad

Serves 10 to 12

Pasta is currently *the* food passion — it's being tossed with everything imaginable. It is also showing up more and more on cold buffet tables as a salad. To make this salad a complete meal, toss in strips of cold cooked ham or cooked shrimp just before serving.

12 ounces spaghettini or vermicelli (300 g)
1 cup grated cheese (250 mL)
1/2 cup sweet pickle relish (125 mL)
2 cups chopped celery (500 mL)
4 hard-cooked eggs, chopped
1 cup mayonnaise (250 mL)
1/2 cup Italian salad dressing (125 mL)
1 teaspoon dry dill (5 mL)
3/4 teaspoon salt (3 mL)
few grindings of freshly ground black pepper

Break the spaghettini or vermicelli in half and boil as directed on the package. Drain thoroughly in a colander and run under cold water *well* to prevent sticking. Add the pasta to a salad bowl along with 3/4 cup (175 mL) of the cheese, the sweet pickle relish, celery and eggs.

Combine the mayonnaise, salad dressing, dill, salt and pepper and pour over the ingredients in the salad bowl. Toss gently with 2 forks until thoroughly mixed. Sprinkle the top of the salad with the remaining grated cheese. This salad is best when served within 1 to 2 hours.

Serve with sliced cold meats, sliced cheese, olives, cherry tomatoes, marinated artichoke hearts and crusty Italian bread.

Orange and Avocado Salad

Serves 4 to 6

So refreshing. The perfect salad to accompany seafood. And you can have the dressing ready a couple of days in advance.

1 orange
1 avocado or papaya
Bibb lettuce, or any soft lettuce (watercress is best if you can find it)
lemon juice

Peel and slice the orange, reserving the peel. Simmer the orange peel until soft. Remove the white membrane with a spoon and discard. Shred the peel. Peel and seed the avocado and slice. Arrange overlapping slices of orange and avocado on a bed of lettuce. Sprinkle the fruit with lemon juice and shredded peel. Refrigerate until serving time. (If you are using avocado, the lemon juice will prevent discoloration for 1 to 2 hours.)

Dressing
2/3 cup salad oil (150 mL)
4 tablespoons orange juice (60 mL)
2 tablespoons lemon juice (30 mL)
1 1/2 tablespoons honey (22 mL)
3/4 teaspoon salt (3 mL)
1 teaspoon paprika (5 mL)
3/4 teaspoon celery seed (3 mL)

Place all the ingredients in a jar. Just before serving, shake well and pour over the salad. This is enough dressing for 3 large oranges and 3 large avocados (or papayas).

Shrimp and Papaya Salad with Curry Dressing

Serves 4

Just the salad to tempt the sophisticated palate. Adjust the amounts depending on the number of people you plan to serve. This can be served as a first course or as a main course at a refreshing summertime luncheon.

1/3 cup mayonnaise (75 mL)
1/2 teaspoon curry powder (2 mL)
4 teaspoons mango chutney* (20 mL)
2 cups diced papaya (500 mL)
2 cups *fresh* shrimp (500 mL)

Combine the mayonnaise, curry and chutney. At serving time, toss with the papaya and shrimp (the little Bay ones are best). Don't toss until just before you are ready to serve, as you want the papaya to retain its own flavor and not absorb any of the shrimp flavor.

* Use the Major Grey type and finely chop any large pieces of mango.

Elise's Minted Pea Salad

Serves 6 to 8

This recipe came to me last summer as I stood on the 18th tee thinking, this is my last chance for a good tee shot! The conversation usually turns to food once we start down the 18th fairway. This salad can be made ahead of time so it's ready to serve while you crow about your eagle!

2 10-ounce packages frozen tiny peas (2 275 g)
1 cup sour cream (250 mL)
1 tablespoon mayonnaise (15 mL)
1 tablespoon sugar (15 mL)
2 green onions, chopped
1/2 teaspoon salt (2 mL)
freshly ground pepper
2 teaspoons chopped fresh mint (10 mL) (see Note)
raw mushroom slices (garnish)

Thaw the peas and drain well. *Do not cook*. Combine the remaining ingredients and toss with the peas. Chill and serve in glass bowl. Garnish with raw mushroom slices.

Note: I use the mint when I am serving the salad with roast lamb or pork. When I serve it with beef or chicken I substitute 6 slices of cooked and crumbled bacon. Sprinkle the bacon on just before serving.

Sliced Tomatoes with Sweet Basil Dressing

Serves 6 to 8

A crusty French loaf is a welcome companion to this salad — you won't want to leave a drop of that delicious dressing.

6 large beefsteak tomatoes
1 cup salad oil (250 mL)
1/4 cup red wine vinegar (60 mL)
1 teaspoon salt (5 mL)
1/2 teaspoon freshly ground black pepper (2 mL)
2 teaspoons sweet basil (10 mL)
2 teaspoons mustard seed mustard (10 mL)
1 teaspoon sugar (5 mL)
1 egg yolk
1 clove garlic, minced
chopped parsley (garnish)
thinly sliced Spanish onions (garnish)

If you have time and the tomatoes are firm, peel them. Slice the tomatoes and place them in a large shallow serving dish.

Place all the remaining ingredients in a jar and shake well. Pour sufficient dressing over the tomatoes to coat the slices and let sit for 1/2 to 1 hour to macerate. Sprinkle the top with freshly chopped parsley — lots of it — just before serving. A few rings of very thinly sliced Spanish onion makes a nice garnish as well.

Store the leftover portion of dressing in the refrigerator and use over any soft leaf lettuce.

Note: If you plant tomatoes in your garden, be sure to put in a few basil plants as well. They really have something going, those two!

The Fourth Hole: Salad Dressings

Creamy Caesar Salad Dressing
1 cup (250 mL)

Pour this dressing over a bowl of chilled romaine lettuce and toss with 2 tablespoons (30 mL) of Parmesan cheese and 1 cup (250 mL) of croutons for a super-tasting "Caesar" salad.

1/2 cup olive oil (125 mL)
2 tablespoons lemon juice (30 mL)
1 teaspoon red wine vinegar (5 mL)
1 small clove garlic, minced
1/4 teaspoon prepared mustard (1 mL)
1/8 teaspoon Worcestershire sauce (0.5 mL)
1 egg
4 capers
1 ounce anchovies (25 g)
1/4 teaspoon salt (1 mL)

Put all the ingredients in a blender and blend for about 20 seconds or until creamy. This dressing will keep in the refrigerator for about a week.

Thousand Island Dressing
1 2/3 cups (400 mL)

1/4 cup chili sauce (60 mL)
3 tablespoons lemon juice (45 mL)
1 tablespoon Worcestershire sauce (15 mL)
1 cup mayonnaise (250 mL)
2 tablespoons minced pimiento-stuffed green olives (30 mL)

Combine all the ingredients and chill.

Marj's French Dressing   2 3/4 cups (675 mL)

There are some excellent commercial dressings on the market, but there are also some super-easy homemade ones. The next time you serve a salad and someone says, "Great dressing! Did you make it?" — you can answer, "Of course."

3/4 cup Mazola oil (175 mL)
1/2 cup sugar (125 mL)
1/2 teaspoon salt (2 mL)
1/8 teaspoon paprika (0.5 mL)
1/2 cup *malt* vinegar (125 mL)
10 ounce can condensed tomato soup (284 mL)

Place all the ingredients in a jar and shake well. This dressing keeps for 2 to 3 weeks in the refrigerator.

Louise's Salad Dressing   1 1/2 cups (375 mL)

When you have four children and one says, "Mom, how about making that salad dressing I like," you have a right to be stumped! I can only respond when it is Louise. The others keep changing their favorites as often as I do.

Toss this dressing with romaine lettuce, croutons and chopped anchovies and you will be complimented on your excellent "Caesar" salad.

3/4 cup salad oil (175 mL)
1/4 cup lemon juice (60 mL)
1 egg yolk
3/4 teaspoon salt (3 mL)
1/4 teaspoon freshly ground black pepper (1 mL)
1/4 teaspoon garlic powder (1 mL)
1 teaspoon Worcestershire sauce (5 mL)
1/4 cup grated Parmesan cheese (60 mL)

Put all the ingredients into blender or food processor and blend until thoroughly mixed.

Mustard Vinaigrette Dressing
3/4 cup (175 mL)

Nice with soft lettuce such as leaf, Bibb, Boston or red lettuce.

1/2 cup oil (125 mL)
2 tablespoons white wine or cider vinegar (30 mL)
1 tablespoon Dijon mustard (15 mL)
1 clove garlic, minced
1/2 teaspoon salt (2 mL)
1/2 teaspoon freshly ground black pepper (2 mL)

Combine all the ingredients and shake in jar.

Dressing for Potato Salad   1 1/2 cups (375 mL)

Quick and easy — my favorite combination for any recipe!

1 cup mayonnaise (250 mL)
1 hard-cooked egg, finely chopped
2 tablespoons red wine vinegar (30 mL)
1 clove garlic, finely minced
1 teaspoon horseradish (5 mL)
1/2 teaspoon salt (2 mL)
1/8 teaspoon black pepper (0.5 mL)

Combine all the ingredients and chill. This recipe makes enough dressing for about 2 pounds (1 kg) of potatoes.

Sunshine Salad Dressing 1 1/2 cups (375 mL)

I am a great salad fan and serve it with great regularity. To keep my family from becoming bored, I am constantly changing the salad dressing. This is a light dressing — very good with soft lettuce such as Boston, Bibb, leaf lettuce or red lettuce. It is also excellent on spinach. Choose a different dressing for coarser lettuce such as iceberg or romaine.

1 cup light salad oil (*not* olive oil or peanut oil) (250 mL)
1/3 cup red wine vinegar (75 mL)
1 tablespoon lemon juice (15 mL)
1 tablespoon soy sauce (15 mL)
2 cloves garlic, minced
1/2 teaspoon paprika (2 mL)
2 teaspoons sugar (10 mL)

Put all the ingredients in a jar and shake well. This dressing will keep 2 to 3 weeks in the refrigerator.

Marion's Yogurt Dressing 1 1/3 cups (325 mL)

There are only 28 calories in 1 tablespoon!

1 cup low fat yogurt (250 mL)
1 tablespoon lemon juice (15 mL)
1/4 cup honey (60 mL)

Put all the ingredients in a bowl and blend.

Note: If you want to serve this with fresh fruit, add 1/4 teaspoon (1 mL) nutmeg and 1/4 teaspoon (1 mL) cinnamon.

ULTRA EASY—SALADS AND SALAD DRESSINGS

Always use canned pineapple for gelatin molds calling for pineapple—if you use fresh, the mold won't gel.

Here are three quick and delicious fruit salad dressings:
1) Add 1 tablespoon (15 mL) of grated orange rind, 1 teaspoon (5 mL) of sugar and 2 drops of Angostura Bitters to 1/2 cup (125 mL) of sour cream and blend well.
2) Stir 2 tablespoons (30 mL) of chopped candied ginger into 1/2 cup (125 mL) of mayonnaise and 1/2 cup (125 mL) of whipping cream.
3) Add grenadine 1 tablespoon (15 mL) at a time to mayonnaise, mixing well to the desired consistency, sweetness and color.

For a twist, sprinkle chow mein noodles over tossed salad instead of croutons.

Always store tomatoes *stem side down*. (This tip comes from a much-respected produce man I know—I can't explain it!)

Advice from my mother—"If you can't make a good fruit salad, don't make one!" She's right. Your fruit salad is only as good as the quality of the fruit you use. You simply can't hide overripe or underripe fruit in a salad.

To improvise a ring mold, place a greased tin can in the center of a well-greased casserole dish.

To serve a tossed salad to a large group, plan on 3 quarts (3 L) of torn-up lettuce for 10 to 12 people.

The Fifth Hole: Sauces

Almost-instant Cheese Sauce
2/3 cup (150 mL)

This is even easier than adding 2 tablespoons (30 mL) of Cheez Whiz to a cup (250 mL) of cream sauce, which I thought was pretty easy. It is excellent over hot cooked broccoli or asparagus.

1/4 cup evaporated milk (60 mL)
1/4 cup grated, sharp Cheddar cheese (60 mL)
2 tablespoons mayonnaise (30 mL)

Heat the milk then stir in the cheese until melted. Remove from the heat and stir in the mayonnaise.
   This sauce reheats well.

Avocado Hollandaise
1 3/4 cups (425 mL)

Great on seafood salad.

1/2 cup butter (125 mL)
2 eggs
1/4 cup lemon juice (60 mL)
1 medium avocado
1/2 teaspoon salt (2 mL)
1/8 teaspoon garlic salt (0.5 mL)
pinch of cayenne

Heat the butter in a small saucepan to bubbling but do not allow to brown.
   Into the container of a blender put the eggs and lemon juice. Turn on the blender and very slowly start adding the butter.
   Peel, seed and cut up the avocado and blend into the butter mixture with the salt, garlic salt and cayenne. Chill. Use within 3 to 4 days.

Cucumber Sauce   2 1/2 cups (375 mL)

Lovely with any cold fish, particularly salmon or trout.

1 medium cucumber, peeled, seeded and finely chopped
1 cup sour cream (250 mL)
2 teaspoons sweet pickle relish (10 mL)
2 teaspoons lemon juice (10 mL)
1 teaspoon finely chopped green onion (5 mL)
salt and freshly ground pepper to taste

Combine all the ingredients and serve cold.

Alison's Cumberland Sauce   1 2/3 (400 mL)

To accompany duck, goose, cold pork — and Liver Pâté (page 14).

zest from 1/2 orange
zest from 1/4 lemon
2 green onions, chopped
1 teaspoon cornstarch (5 mL)
1 cup dry port (250 mL)
1/2 cup red currant jelly (125 mL)

Cut the zests into narrow strips and boil them for 15 minutes. Drain. In a small saucepan of water simmer the green onions until soft. Drain, pressing out all moisture. Mix the cornstarch and port and combine in a saucepan with the orange and lemon zests, the green onions and the red currant jelly. Simmer until clear.
   Serve hot or cold.

Hollandaise Sauce   1 cup (250 mL)

This isn't one of those mock hollandaise sauces with mayonnaise or sour cream, it is the real McCoy, with all of the original, essential ingredients. The secret (disclosed to me by a lovely lady at CJRT–FM Toronto) is to put everything into the pot *cold*. Thank you Diane!

juice of 1 lemon
1/2 cup butter (125 mL)
2 egg yolks
1/4 teaspoon salt (1 mL)
pinch of cayenne

Place all of the ingredients in a small saucepan and heat *slowly* while stirring constantly, until thickened.

Serve warm over poached eggs, or over cooked broccoli or asparagus.

Note: Should the sauce curdle (a too-high heat will do this) immediately stir in an ice cube.

Lorraine's Curry Dressing for Seafood
1 1/4 cups (310 mL)

1 cup mayonnaise or salad dressing (250 mL)
2 teaspoons curry powder (10 mL)
1/4 cup milk (60 mL)
1 clove garlic, minced
1/4 teaspoon Worcestershire sauce (1 mL)
6 to 8 drops Tabasco sauce

Mix all ingredients and chill. Serve on chilled seafood.

Quick Horseradish Sauce
1/3 cup (75 mL)

Wonderful with cold corned beef or roast beef. You can make any quantity of this easy sauce simply by combining equal amounts of the ingredients.

2 tablespoons mayonnaise (30 mL)
2 tablespoons sour cream (30 mL)
2 tablespoons horseradish (30 mL)
pinch of salt and pepper

Combine all the above ingredients. Serve cold.

Favorite Sauce for Lamb About 1 cup (250 mL)

For those who find mint sauce too vinegary and mint jelly too sweet, here is a perfect compromise!

1/2 cup mint sauce (125 mL)
1/3 cup black or red currant jelly (75 mL)
1/3 cup chili sauce (75 mL)

Put all the ingredients in a small saucepan and heat until the jelly melts. Serve hot or cold.
   This sauce will keep for 4 to 6 weeks in the refrigerator.

Mushroom Sauce 2 cups (500 mL)

A useful little sauce to dress up meat loaf, pork chops, cutlets, even baked fish.

1/2 pound fresh mushrooms (225 g)
1/4 cup minced onion (60 mL)
2 tablespoons butter (30 mL)
2 tablespoons flour (30 mL)
1/2 cup cereal cream (125 mL)
1/2 teaspoon salt (2 mL)
pinch of pepper
1/4 teaspoon Worcestershire sauce (1 mL)
1/2 cup sour cream (125 mL)

Slice the mushrooms and sauté them in butter along with the onions until tender, but not brown. Sprinkle with the flour and stir. Gradually stir in the cream and simmer until thickened. Stir in the salt, pepper and Worcestershire sauce. Remove from the heat and stir in the sour cream.

Note: This sauce may be made ahead and reheated, but do not allow it to boil or the sour cream will curdle. See Poor Man's Beef Wellington for an alternate Mushroom Sauce.

Quick Mustard Sauce

1/3 cup (75 mL)

We sometimes refer to this as Ted's Mustard in honor of our architect in-law.

2 tablespoons mayonnaise (30 mL)
2 tablespoons brown sugar (30 mL)
2 tablespoons hot mustard (30 mL)
2 tablespoons horseradish (30 mL)

Combine all the ingredients. This makes 1/3 cup (75 mL) but you can make any amount you wish by mixing equal amounts of the ingredients.

Serve cold with ham, corned beef or cold roast beef. It is also nice with grilled or sautéed liver.

Seafood Cocktail Sauce

1 cup (250 mL)

Here's an old favorite for shrimp and raw oysters.

1/2 cup ketchup (125 mL)
1/2 cup chili sauce (125 mL)
1 tablespoon horseradish (15 mL)
1 teaspoon Worcestershire sauce (5 mL)
1 teaspoon lemon juice (5 mL)
few drops of Tabasco

Combine all the ingredients and chill. This will keep well for several weeks in refrigerator.

Apricot Sauce

1 1/4 cups (310 mL)

This sauce may be made ahead and warmed slightly before serving.

1 cup apricot jam (250 mL)
1 tablespoon water (15 mL)
1/4 cup apricot brandy (60 mL)

Slowly bring the jam and water to a boil in a small saucepan. Remove from the heat and stir in the brandy. Press through a strainer.

Serve warm over vanilla ice cream or over a fresh slice of pound cake. Sprinkle toasted almonds on top.

Jean's Chocolate Sauce
1 1/2 cups (375 mL)

The sauce will harden slightly on the cold ice cream — very addicting.

1 1/2 squares unsweetened chocolate
1/2 cup boiling water (125 mL)
1 tablespoon butter (15 mL)
1 cup sugar (250 mL)
1/2 teaspoon vanilla (2 mL)

Melt the chocolate over hot water or in a saucepan over very low heat. Add the boiling water, butter and sugar, stirring constantly. Boil for 3 minutes. Remove from the heat and stir in the vanilla.
   Spoon hot over ice cream.

Note: Two tablespoons (30 mL) of corn syrup must be added if you intend to store this sauce in the refrigerator, or it will turn sugary. I seldom do this as this recipe makes 4 generous servings and we use it all — just as quickly as we can get it from the pot onto our ice cream!

Hot Rum Sauce
2 3/4 cups (675 mL)

1 cup maple syrup (250 mL)
1/2 cup light corn syrup (125 mL)
1 cup walnuts, coarsely chopped (250 mL)
1/4 cup dark rum (60 mL)

In a small saucepan combine the syrups. Bring to a boil. Reduce the heat and simmer for 5 minutes. Remove from the heat and stir in the nuts and rum.
   Serve hot over ice cream or cold over hot apple pie, mincemeat pie or whatever suits your fancy.

Gilley Grand Marnier Sauce

3 1/3 cups (825 mL)

Sensational over fresh strawberries — or any fresh fruit.

2 cups milk (500 mL)
1/4 cup butter (60 mL)
2/3 cup sugar (150 mL)
3 egg yolks (have at room temperature)
2 tablespoons cornstarch (30 mL)
1 teaspoon vanilla (5 mL)
1/3 cup whipping cream (75 mL)
1/3 cup Grand Marnier (75 mL)

Combine the milk, butter, and 1/3 cup (75 mL) of the sugar in a saucepan. Bring to a boil, stirring occasionally.

In a mixer, beat the egg yolks until thickened. Add the cornstarch and the remaining 1/3 cup (75 mL) of sugar. Beat until lemon colored. Beat *some* of the hot milk into the egg mixture (to warm). Add the egg mixture to the milk and whisk until blended. Bring to a boil while continuing to stir.

Remove from the heat. Blend in the vanilla, whipping cream and Grand Marnier.

Serve hot or cold.

ULTRA EASY — SAUCES

Need a "hurry up" white sauce? Tear 3 slices of white bread and put the pieces into a blender with 1 cup (250 mL) of hot milk, 1/4 teaspoon (1 mL) of salt and a pinch each of white pepper and cayenne. Blend for 20 seconds.

Here are four quickie dipping sauces for raw vegetables or meat fondue: To mayonnaise add 1) a bit of prepared mustard; 2) tomato ketchup; 3) a bit of horseradish; and 4) curry powder to taste!

You can make a very easy and versatile sauce for cauliflower by combining a 10 ounce (284 mL) can of condensed cream of mushroom soup mixed with 1/2 cup (125 mL) of sour cream and *one* of the following (depending on your mood and resources): 1 cup (250 mL) grated Cheddar cheese, 1 cup (250 mL) sautéed fresh mushrooms, 1 can small shrimp, well drained. Cook a cauliflower until tender-crisp, drain, pour your sauce over it and finish the cooking in a 350°F (180°C) oven — 20 to 30 minutes should do it.

Apricot jam thinned with orange juice makes a very nice sauce for French toast. And you can serve a gourmet breakfast by making the French toast in the following slightly different manner: Make sandwiches with a filling of cream cheese and chopped walnuts, dip the sandwiches in your favorite egg mixture and fry them, then serve them with the apricot jam-orange juice sauce.

For a "hurry up" chocolate sauce, blend a 6 ounce (175 g) package of chocolate chips with 1 cup (250 mL) of heavy cream in the top of a double boiler. When the chips and cream are well blended, stir in 1 1/2 to 2 tablespoons (22 mL to 30 mL) of rum, Amaretto or Grand Marnier.

The Sixth Hole: Fish and Seafood

Broiled Salmon Steaks with Sour Cream and Dill

Serves 4

4 1-inch salmon steaks (2.5 cm)
3 tablespoons butter (45 mL)
salt and pepper

Sour Cream and Dill Sauce
1 1/2 cups sour cream (372 mL)
1 1/2 tablespoons lemon juice (22 mL)
pinch of salt
pinch of pepper
2 green onions, finely chopped
1 teaspoon dill (5 mL)

Brush the salmon steaks with butter on both sides and sprinkle them with salt and pepper. Broil them for 3 minutes on one side, turn, brush with additional butter and broil for an additional 3 minutes. *Do not overcook.*

Combine the sauce ingredients in a small saucepan. Heat but do not allow to boil. Pour sauce over the fish and serve immediately.

Tiny new potatoes, glazed cucumbers and tomato halves filled with puréed peas are a nice accompaniment. (Purée undercooked peas in a food processor with a pinch of the cooking water, 1 to 2 tablespoons — 15 to 30 mL of butter, a pinch of salt and a pinch of sugar.)

Linguini·with Clam Sauce

Serves 4

Just recently I was making Linguini with Crab Sauce. My youngest daughter arrived home with the usual "What's for dinner, Mom?" When I told her, the reply was, "I'd rather have clam sauce." I took this page from the manuscript, handed it to her and said, "Alright, make it!" She did and we *all* had both.

If you keep 2 cans of clams and a box of linguini on your emergency shelf — you usually have the remaining ingredients on hand.

1/4 cup *olive* oil (60 mL)
2 tablespoons butter (30 mL)
3 large cloves of garlic, minced
1/4 cup chopped *fresh* parsley (60 mL)
1/4 teaspoon crushed dried red chili peppers (1 mL)
2 5-ounce cans baby clams, drained (2 147 g)
1/4 cup dry white wine (60 mL)
1/4 cup freshly grated Parmesan cheese (60 mL)
hot cooked linguini (see Note)
2 chopped green onions (garnish)

Put the oil, butter, garlic, 2 tablespoons (30 mL) of the parsley and the chili pepper in a skillet. Cook for 2 minutes. Add the clams and wine and cook for 5 minutes, uncovered. Add the Parmesan cheese and the remaining parsley. Remove from the heat and toss with hot cooked linguini. Garnish with chopped green onions.

Note: One pound (450 g) of linguini is sufficient for 6 people. I would suggest cooking about 2/3 this amount for the amount of sauce above.

Serve with a tossed green salad or a Caesar salad, crusty buns or a good quality French loaf and a fresh fruit plate for dessert.

Helpful Hint: There are inexpensive acrylic cheese grinders available for you pasta lovers. Freshly grated Parmesan is *so* superior to the hand shaker, pregrated cheese we always reach for. It really is worth that extra "twist of the wrist," which is all that it takes to grate your own.

Fish Fillets — Fried or Baked   Serves 4 to 5

Not everyone's budget will allow a steady diet of shellfish. The less expensive fish, such as cod, Boston Bluefish and ocean perch, are very respectable and should not be overlooked.

1 1/2 pounds fish fillets (750 g)

Fried
1/2 to 3/4 cup flour, seasoned with garlic salt and pepper
(125 mL to 180 mL)
1/4 cup unsalted butter (60 mL)
OR
2 tablespoons each of butter and oil (30 mL)

Dip the fillets in the seasoned flour and fry them in the unsalted butter (or butter and oil) until browned on both sides. Remove to a warmed platter. To the skillet in which the fish was browned add 2 tablespoons (30 mL) butter. When the butter is bubbly, add the following:

1/4 cup white wine vinegar (60 mL)
1/2 teaspoon dillweed (2 mL)
2 tablespoons chopped fresh parsley (30 mL)

Bring this sauce to a boil, stirring constantly and scraping up drippings from the fish. Simmer for about 2 minutes then pour over the cooked fillets and serve.

Baked
3 tablespoons butter (45 mL)
1/4 cup white wine vinegar (60 mL)
1/8 teaspoon garlic powder (0.5 mL)
1/2 teaspoon dillweed (2 mL)

Arrange the fillets in a shallow buttered baking dish in a single layer. Overlap the thinnest portions or tuck thin ends under so the fish will cook evenly. Melt the butter in a small skillet and add the remaining ingredients. Stir until well blended then pour over the fish fillets. Bake in a preheated 350°F (180°C) oven for 15 minutes or until the fish flakes easily with a fork. *Do not overcook.*

Serve either Fried or Baked Fish with French-fried potatoes, green beans and a salad.

Elegant Crab and Shrimp   Serves 8

Very impressive, whichever presentation you choose. The individual pastry casseroles make a lovely fish course at a special dinner party. The cream puff ring is perfect for a luncheon.

Crab and Shrimp Filling
10 ounce can condensed cream of shrimp soup (284 mL)
2 tablespoons sherry (30 mL)
1/4 cup cream (60 mL)
1/3 cup grated Swiss cheese (75 mL)

1 pound fresh or frozen crabmeat (450 g)
   OR
2 7-ounce cans crabmeat (2-198 g)
1 pound cooked shrimp (*not* canned) (450 g)

In a saucepan combine the soup, sherry and cream. Heat the mixture to bubbling. Stir in the cheese and fish and continue to simmer until the cheese has melted and the fish is heated through.

Spoon the mixture *either* into the individual pastry casseroles *or* the cream puff ring.

Pastry Casseroles
14 ounce package frozen puff pastry (397 g)

Thaw the puff pastry according to the directions on the package. Divide the dough into 9 equal pieces. Roll out thinly 8 7-inch (18 cm) circles. Roll out the ninth portion of dough and cut it into 8 narrow strips to make "handles."

Line 8 tart pans, 4 1/2 inches (11.5 cm) in diameter, with the circles. Press the dough firmly against the edges of the pans and prick it with a fork. Line each pan with waxed paper and weight it with some rice or dried beans.

Bake the shells and handles in a 400°F (200°C) oven — 6 to 8 minutes for the handles, 12 minutes for the shells. Discard the waxed paper and rice or beans and continue baking the shells for an additional 3 to 5 minutes or until golden brown.

Spoon the Crab and Shrimp Filling into the shells. Place the handles so that just the tips touch the filling. Serve hot.

Cream Puff Ring

Follow the recipe for Cream Puff Shells on page 196, *substituting* 3 ounces (75 g) of grated Swiss cheese for the tablespoon (15 mL) of sugar called for in the recipe. Form all the dough into a ring (instead of individual servings). Bake the ring on a cookie sheet. When the ring has cooled, split it in half and fill it with the crab and shrimp mixture.

For a luncheon, serve the ring with peas sautéed with fresh mushrooms, a tossed green salad and a lemon dessert.

Note: The ring can be made ahead and frozen. Thaw, then fill just before serving.

Crisp Crusted Oysters
Serves 3 to 4

I adore oysters and rarely cook them as I prefer them raw—but when I do, this is one of my favorite methods.

3 tablespoons flour (45 mL)
dash of black pepper
1/4 teaspoon nutmeg (1 mL)
1 pound West Coast oysters* (450 g)
1 egg, slightly beaten
1/2 cup cornflake crumbs (125 mL)
2 tablespoons butter (30 mL)
2 tablespoons oil (30 mL)

Combine the flour with the pepper and nutmeg. Coat the oysters with this mixture and let them dry for 15 minutes.

Dip the oysters in the slightly beaten egg and then in the cornflake crumbs. Let stand an additional 15 minutes to dry the crust.

Sauté the oysters in the butter and oil until golden. Serve with lemon wedges.

Creamed spinach, tossed salad and cheese bread are a nice accompaniment to this dish.

* West Coast oysters are larger than those harvested on the East Coast.

Steamed Salmon Steaks with Anchovy Lemon Butter

Serves 4

4 salmon steaks
2 tablespoons minced onion (30 mL)
salt and pepper

Set the salmon steaks on heavy aluminum in single layer. Sprinkle them with the onions and salt and pepper. Turn up the edges of the foil to catch the juice but do not wrap tightly. Pour 1/2 inch (12 mm) of water in large shallow pan and bring to boil. Lift the salmon on the foil into the pan, being careful that the foil keeps the water from touching the fish. Turn the heat down. *Cover the pan* and simmer for about 20 minutes (depending on the thickness of the fish) or until the salmon flakes with a fork. Do not overcook.

Anchovy Lemon Butter
1/4 pound butter (unsalted if you have it) (125 g)
1/4 cup lemon juice (60 mL)
2 tablespoons anchovy paste (30 mL)

Heat all the ingredients together in a small saucepan and pour over the cooked salmon steaks. Serve immediately.

Note: Anchovy Butter is also great on broiled salmon steaks. Spoon some sauce over the steaks, broil for 3 minutes on one side, turn, spoon additional sauce over the fish and broil for an additional 3 minutes. Remove to a heated platter and spoon any remaining sauce over. Serve with lemon wedges.

Shrimp and Chicken Breast in Tomato Sauce

Serves 4 to 6

From a friend in San Francisco, via New York and Portland. When I see a recipe calling for 1 or 2 tablespoons of tomato paste, I immediately think, "What am I supposed to do with the rest of the can?" This recipe is so good — who cares? (I actually *do* care — so see the Note at the bottom).

The sauce can be made in the morning, then it takes no time to assemble the remainder of dish.

1 tablespoon oil (15 mL)
1/3 cup finely chopped celery (75 mL)
1/3 cup finely chopped carrots (75 mL)
1/2 cup finely chopped onion (125 mL)
1/2 teaspoon finely minced garlic (2 mL)
4 teaspoons finely minced shallots (20 mL)
2 cups crushed tomatoes (500 mL)
2 tablespoons tomato paste (30 mL)
1/2 cup dry white wine (125 mL)
1/2 teaspoon dried tarragon (2 mL)
salt and pepper to taste
2 tablespoons butter (30 mL)
1 pound skinless, boneless chicken breast, (450 g)
  cut into 1 inch strips (2.5 cm)
1 pound uncooked shrimp, large size (450 g)
2 tablespoons cognac (30 mL)
1 teaspoon finely chopped parsley (5 mL)

Heat the oil in a saucepan. Add the celery, carrots, onions, garlic and 1 teaspoon (5 ml) of the minced shallots. Cook, stirring briefly until the onion is wilted. Add the tomatoes, tomato paste, wine and 1/4 teaspoon (1 mL) dried tarragon. Add salt and pepper to taste. Bring to a boil and simmer for 15 minutes. Set aside.

Heat the butter until hot and add the cut-up chicken breasts with a few shakes of salt and pepper. Cook for about 45 seconds. Add the shrimp and stir. Cook 1 minute. Add the remaining shallots and cognac. Add the remaining tarragon, the parsley and the tomato sauce you have set aside. Bring to a boil and simmer for just a few minutes.

Note: You can freeze the leftover tomato paste by lining a baking sheet with waxed paper and dropping tomato paste by tablespoonfuls (15 mL measures) onto the paper. Place in freezer and when solidly frozen, remove from the waxed paper and place in plastic bags. Store in freezer. It is all measured when you need it!

Try wild rice and green beans almondine as accompaniments.

Lynn's Scallops in Lime Ginger Cream
Serves 6

One of life's biggest treats for me is to go to my daughter Lynn's for dinner. If my two younger girls turn out to be as accomplished in the kitchen as their elder sister, my waistline is in big trouble — more trouble than it already is!

1 1/2 pounds scallops (750 g)
1/2 cup cornstarch (125 mL)
6 tablespoons butter (90 mL)
1 tablespoon grated fresh ginger (15 mL)
2 green onions, sliced
grated rind of 1 lime
2 tablespoons lime juice (30 mL)
1 1/2 cups chicken bouillon or fish stock (375 mL)
1 cup heavy cream (250 mL)

Dust the scallops with cornstarch. Melt 5 tablespoons (75 mL) of the butter in a large skillet and sauté the scallops for 5 minutes. Remove the scallops with a slotted spoon to a heated platter to keep warm and pour the excess fat from pan.

Add the remaining 1 tablespoon (15 mL) of butter to pan and sauté the ginger, green onion and grated lime for 2 minutes. Add the lime juice, bouillon and cream. Bring to a boil and continue boiling until slightly reduced. Return the scallops to the pan and simmer, stirring frequently until the sauce is thickened.

Serve at once over cooked, drained linguini.

Note: I would not suggest making the scallops ahead of time, but the linguini can be cooked ahead and reheated by simply pouring boiling water over it!

A tossed green salad and crusty Italian loaf are all the accompaniments you need.

Shrimp and Mushroom Broil

Serves 4

This makes a very easy dinner. Most supermarkets carry the bamboo skewers now. The only secret is to soak the skewers in cold water before using. If you use the metal skewers, which are longer, and an outside barbecue, you can liven this dish up with additions of cherry tomatoes and pieces of green pepper.

If I am *trying* to diet and have to entertain, this is one of my favorite things to serve (and I serve it with my old standby favorite low-cal dessert — Dieter's Delight on page 192).

1/2 cup oil (125 mL)
1/4 cup dry vermouth (60 mL)
3 tablespoons light soy sauce (45 mL)
1/4 teaspoon powdered ginger (1 mL)
1 clove garlic, minced
2 pounds raw *large* shrimp, shelled and deveined (1 kg)
1/2 pound fresh mushrooms (225 g)

Combine the oil, vermouth, soy sauce, ginger and garlic. Marinate the shrimp in this for 20 to 30 minutes. Thread the shrimp onto bamboo skewers alternately with mushrooms. Broil, turning and basting with marinade, for 5 minutes.

Nice accompanied by stir-fried Chinese vegetables.

Curried Shrimp

Serves 4

For some reason spicy foods and hot weather are a natural match. When I have a hot match, this is a dish I like to come home to. I make the sauce the night before, then reheat it and add the shrimp at serving time.

1/4 cup margarine (60 mL)
1/4 cup finely chopped onion (60 mL)
1 clove garlic, crushed
1/2 cup tart apple, peeled and chopped (125 mL)
2 teaspoons curry powder (10 mL)
1/4 cup flour (60 mL)
10 ounce can chicken broth, undiluted (284 mL)
1/2 cup cereal cream (125 mL)
1 pound shrimp, cooked (450 g)
1/4 cup golden raisins (60 mL)
salt and pepper to taste

Melt the margarine and sauté the onions, garlic and apple until tender but not brown. Stir in the curry powder and flour. Blend well. Stir in the chicken broth and cereal cream. Cook, stirring constantly until thickened. Add the shrimp and raisins. Season to taste with salt and pepper.
　Serve over hot rice.

Chopped banana, peanuts, chutney and fresh coconut chips are sumptuous toppings.

Sole Florentine

Serves 4

If you like to serve fish, and in a hurry, you certainly should know about this little gem.

1 pound sole fillets (450 g)
1 package Stouffer's Frozen Spinach Soufflé
4 slices bacon
2 tablespoons melted butter (30 mL)
3/4 cup crushed rice flakes (175 mL)

If frozen, thaw the sole and dry well with paper towels, as frozen fish tends to be watery. Thaw the spinach soufflé. Cook the bacon until crisp and set aside. Crumble when cool.

Place the sole in a buttered shallow baking dish 7 by 12 inch — 18 cm × 30 cm or 8 inch square — 1.2 L. Spoon the soufflé on top of the fillets (don't spread it too thinly—leave about a 1 inch or 2.5 cm border of fish showing around the edges).

Combine the melted butter and rice flakes and sprinkle all over the top of the dish. Top this with the crumbled bacon. Bake in a preheated 400°F (200°C) oven for 15 to 20 minutes, or until the fish flakes easily with a fork.

Whole cherry tomatoes or broiled tomato halves and a box of long grain and wild rice mix are easy accompaniments.

Pan-fried Brook Trout   Serves 4

If you have decided to go fishing instead of golfing over the weekend, be sure to take along some cornmeal and a slab of bacon!

4 whole trout
salt and pepper
8 slices bacon
2 cups cornmeal (500 mL)

Clean the trout but do not remove the heads and tails. Rinse the fish under the cold water tap. Dry thoroughly. Sprinkle inside and out with salt and pepper.

Cook the bacon in a large skillet and remove to paper towels. Leave the drippings in the skillet.

Dip the fish in cornmeal then fry them in the bacon fat for 4 to 5 minutes on each side.

Serve at once, garnished with lemon wedges, parsley and strips of bacon.

Small potato balls and fried green tomatoes will complement the trout nicely.

Smothered Shrimp

Serves 4 to 5

---

12 to 16 ounces *fresh or frozen* medium to large shrimp (400 g)
1 medium onion, finely chopped
1/2 cup finely chopped celery (125 mL)
6 tablespoons butter (90 mL)
6 ounce can crabmeat, drained (170 g)
1 1/2 tablespoons dry sherry (22 mL)
2 tablespoons flour (30 mL)
1/4 teaspoon dry mustard (1 mL)
1 cup milk (250 mL)
2 tablespoons Miracle Whip (30 mL)
1/4 teaspoon Worcestershire sauce (1 mL)
1/2 teaspoon salt (2 mL)
Parmesan cheese

If frozen, thaw the shrimp. Split the shrimp and open them flat. Place the shrimp in a single layer in a shallow baking dish.

Sauté the onions and celery in 4 tablespoons (60 mL) of the butter. Add the crabmeat and sherry and stir.

Melt the remaining 2 tablespoons (30 mL) of butter in a small saucepan. Blend in the flour and dry mustard. Stir in the milk and cook, stirring until thickened. Add the Miracle Whip, Worcestershire sauce and salt. Combine with the crabmeat mixture. (At this point the shrimp and sauce may be refrigerated. Finish preparing the dish and bake it in the evening just before serving.)

Spoon all over the shrimp and dot with extra butter. Sprinkle lightly with Parmesan cheese. Bake in a 350°F (180°C) oven for 20 to 25 minutes.

Serve with hot saffron rice and a tossed green salad.

Slightly Oriental Sole

Serves 3 to 4

The sauce can be made before you go golfing, then reheated and poured over the fillets before you place them in the oven. You even have time to stay for coffee after the game and brag about all of your fine shots — if you can find anyone who will listen!

1 pound fresh sole fillets (450 g)
1/4 cup butter (60 mL)
1/4 pound mushrooms, sliced (110 g)
1 tablespoon cornstarch (15 mL)
1/4 teaspoon ground ginger (1 mL)
2 tablespoons cold water (30 mL)
1 cup boiling water (250 mL)
1 1/2 tablespoons soy sauce (22 mL)
1 1/2 tablespoons ketchup (22 mL)

Place the sole in a well-buttered flat baking dish.

In a medium-sized saucepan, melt the butter and sauté the mushrooms until soft.

Combine the cornstarch, ginger and cold water. When smooth, combine with the boiling water, soya sauce and ketchup. Add this mixture to the mushrooms and simmer all together until slightly thickened. Pour over the sole and bake in a 400°F (200°C) oven for 20 to 25 minutes.

Serve with hot fluffy rice and a tossed green salad. Be sure to include some tomatoes, green pepper and fresh bean sprouts in your salad.

ULTRA EASY — FISH AND SEAFOOD

To given frozen fish a fresher flavor, thaw it in milk. Drain it before cooking.

For a quick dinner for one, drain a small can of salmon and place it in a baking dish. Top the fish with 1/2 cup (125 mL) of sour cream and bake in a 325°F (160°C) oven until the cream turns golden — 20 to 25 minutes is about right.

To bread fish for frying, always use bread crumbs rather than cracker crumbs. The bread absorbs much less grease.

Use peanut oil for deep-fat frying because it burns at a higher temperature than ordinary vegetable oil.

To freeze salmon, rub it with lemon juice first and the thawed fish will taste fresher.

Turn a simple sole dish into Sole Veronique by making this easy sauce: Combine 1/4 cup (60 mL) of butter, 1/2 cup (125 mL) of white wine and 1 cup (250 mL) of green grapes and simmer for about 8 minutes. Pour the sauce over broiled sole.

The Seventh Hole:
Meat

Marinated Flank Steak   Serves 4

This is a fairly regular feature during the summer months. I let it sit in
the marinade while I am out parring the course . . . ? When I come home it
is all ready to place under the broiler. Stir-fried vegetables and cheese
bread make nice accompaniments.

2 pounds flank steak (1 kg)
3 tablespoons oil (45 mL)
4 tablespoons soy sauce (60 mL)
2 teaspoons brown sugar (10 mL)
1/4 teaspoon ground ginger (1 mL)
1/4 teaspoon pepper (1 mL)
1 clove garlic, minced
no salt

Remove as much membrane from the steak as possible. Score the meat
on both sides. Mix the remaining ingredients and pour over the meat.
Let the steak marinate for about 3 hours at room temperature.

Broil for 5 minutes on one side and 4 minutes on the other. It will be
medium rare. Broiled flank steak should not be too rare or too well
done.

Serve thinly sliced against the grain.

Broiled Ginger Steak

Serves 4

A specialty of my brother David. If I know he is coming to visit, I make sure I have fresh ginger and a lovely big sirloin steak on hand. Don't use too much ginger as it is very strong.

3/4 cup red wine (175 mL)
1/4 cup soy sauce (60 mL)
2 or 3 cloves garlic, minced
1/2 inch to 1 inch piece of fresh ginger, finely minced (1 cm to 2.5 cm)
2 pounds sirloin steak (1 kg)

Combine the first 4 ingredients and marinate the steak in this mixture for 2 hours.

Broil or barbecue the steak to a desired degree of doneness, basting with marinade as it cooks. Slice thinly against the grain. If the meat was broiled, pour the pan juices over before serving.

Serve with carrots, snow pea pods and garlic bread.

Eye of the Round Roast of Beef

Serves 6

This is sometimes referred to as a shell-bone roast. It is a particular favorite of mine for it is quite lean and easy to carve and the timing is very accurate. If you have any leftover red wine, make your own marinade rather than buying the bottled dressing. Use 3 parts wine to 1 part olive oil and add garlic salt and lots of freshly ground black pepper.

3 to 4 pound eye of the round roast (1.5 kg to 2 kg)
8 ounce bottle of Italian salad dressing (250 mL)

Marinate the roast in the dressing for 2 to 3 days, turning occasionally. Keep refrigerated.

Roast for 1 hour in a 350°F (180°C) oven for rare.

Roast for 1 hour in a 400°F (200°C) oven for medium-rare.

Slice against the grain and serve with artichoke bottoms filled with béarnaise sauce for an elegant meal. Duchess potatoes and baby carrots plus the Overnight Layered Salad on page 38 would be the perfect ending to a perfect day — or even a not so perfect day!

Beef Stroganoff

The following method is for those who like their steak rare or medium-rare. Cooking the steak first is a good way of ensuring your steak will be the way you like it — plus providing easier slicing.

1 1/2 pounds beef tenderloin (750 g)
3 tablespoons butter (45 mL)
1 medium onion, thinly sliced
1/4 pound fresh mushrooms, sliced (110 g)
2 tablespoons flour (30 mL)
10 ounce can beef bouillon (284 mL)
2 tablespoons tomato paste (30 mL)
2 teaspoons Worcestershire sauce (10 mL)
1/2 teaspoon dry mustard (2 mL)
1/2 teaspoon salt (2 mL)
1/4 teaspoon freshly ground black pepper (1 mL)
1 cup sour cream (250 mL)
3 tablespoons sherry (45 mL)

Salt and pepper the tenderloin and brown it in 1 tablespoon (15 mL) of the butter until desired doneness — remember it will cook just a little more when it sits in the hot sauce, but not much. Let the steak cool and slice it in 1/4 inch (7 mm) slices about 2 inches (5 cm) long.

Add the remaining 2 tablespoons (30 mL) of butter to the skillet and sauté the onions and mushrooms until the onion is soft. Sprinkle the vegetables with flour and blend in. Add the bouillon, tomato paste, Worcestershire sauce, dry mustard, salt and pepper. Cook, stirring constantly until thickened. Stir in the sour cream, sherry and beef. Heat thoroughly but do not allow to boil.

Serve over hot cooked noodles, tossed with 1 to 2 tablespoons (15 to 30 mL) of butter and 1 1/2 teaspoons (7 mL) of poppy seed.

Stir-fried Beef with Tomatoes

Serves 4

This is one of Wayne Gretzky's favorite dishes *and* did you know he is an avid golfer?

1 1/2 pounds flank steak (750 g)
2 tablespoons oil (30 mL)
3 tomatoes, cut into eighths
4 green onions, cut into 1 inch pieces (2.5 cm)
2 tablespoons soy sauce (30 mL)
2 teaspoons cornstarch (10 mL)

Marinate the flank steak as for Marinated Flank Steak on page 71. Remove the steak from the marinade and slice it thinly against the grain.

In an electric fry pan or wok heat the oil. Add the beef and quickly stir-fry over high heat for 2 to 3 minutes. Add the tomatoes and onions and stir them along with the meat, just long enough to heat them—you don't want to cook them. This will only take about 1 minute. Blend the cornstarch and soy sauce and stir this into the mixture. Cook for 1 minute.

Serve immediately over hot cooked rice.

Individual Beef Wellingtons with Escargot Sauce

Serves 8

The Wellingtons may be prepared a day or two before your party and stored in the refrigerator until baking time. The sauce can be prepared in advance too and reheated, so this elegant meal really leaves you lots of time to enjoy your guests.

4 tablespoons butter (60 mL)
8 beef tenderloin fillets, 4 to 6 ounces each (125 g to 175 g)
salt and pepper
1 clove garlic
1 cup chopped mushrooms (250 mL)
2 4-ounce cans liver pâté (2 125 g)
frozen puff pastry — enough for 8 8-inch squares (20 cm)

Melt the butter. Sprinkle the fillets with salt and pepper and rub each with a cut clove of garlic. Sear the steaks on both sides—very quickly if you like your steak rare. If you prefer a medium steak, cook 2 minutes on each side; for well done, cook 4 minutes on each side. Chill.

To the pan drippings add the chopped mushrooms and sauté until wilted. Remove from the heat and mix with the liver pâté. When the steaks are chilled, spread the tops with the liver pâté-mushroom mixture.

Roll out the pastry according to the directions on the package and cut it into 8 8-inch (20 cm) squares. Place each fillet in the middle of a square of pastry, pâté side down. Bring the edges up over the fillet and moisten with water to seal. Place the wrapped fillets seam side down on a greased cookie sheet. Prick the pastry with a fork. Any leftover scraps of dough may be cut with scissors to make designs for the tops of the Wellingtons. If you do this, brush the tops with beaten egg. Bake in a 425°F (220°C) oven for 30 minutes or until the pastry is cooked. Serve with Escargot Sauce.

Escargot Sauce
3 tablespoons butter (45 mL)
4 green onions, finely chopped
1/2 clove garlic, minced
1 tablespoon flour (15 mL)
1 tablespoon Bisto (15 mL)
10 ounce can beef broth (284 mL)
3/4 cup red wine (175 mL)
4 1/2 ounce can escargots, drained (140 g)

Melt the butter and sauté the onions and garlic until soft. Sprinkle with flour and Bisto and blend in. Gradually add the broth and wine and cook, stirring until thickened. Stir in the escargots and simmer them in the sauce until heated through. Pass the sauce separately.

Alison's Make-ahead Casserole   Serves 6

This is really a Greek dish, named "Pastitsio." It can be assembled ahead of time — in the morning or the night before.

1 medium onion, chopped
1 clove garlic, minced
2 tablespoons olive oil (30 mL)
1 1/2 pounds ground beef (750 g)
1 teaspoon salt (5 mL)
7 1/2 ounce can tomato sauce (213 mL)
2 dashes cinnamon
1 1/4 cups dry macaroni (300 mL)
2 eggs
2 tablespoons margarine (30 mL)
2 cups grated Cheddar cheese (500 mL)

Cream Sauce
3 tablespoons margarine (45 mL)
1/4 cup flour (60 mL)
2 cups milk (500 mL)
1/2 teaspoon salt (2 mL)
dash of pepper
dash of nutmeg
1/3 cup grated Parmesan cheese (75 mL)

Sauté the onion and garlic in the oil until soft. Add the ground beef and salt and sauté until the pink disappears from the meat. Drain off the fat. Stir in tomato sauce and cinnamon. Set aside while you make the cream sauce.

Melt the margarine in a saucepan and stir in the flour. Gradually add the milk and cook until thickened. Stir in the salt, pepper, nutmeg and Parmesan.

Cook the macaroni, drain and return to the pan. Break in the eggs and add 2 tablespoons (30 mL) of margarine. Mix well.

Butter a large casserole dish and layer the ingredients thus—half the macaroni, all of the meat, half the grated Cheddar cheese, the remaining macaroni, then all the cream sauce. Shake the dish very gently. Sprinkle on the remaining Cheddar cheese. Dot the top with butter and a few sprinkles of nutmeg.

Bake in a preheated 375°F (190°C) oven for 45 minutes. If made ahead and refrigerated, allow an extra 15 minutes in the oven.

Serve with Greek Salad and cheese or garlic bread.

Sweet and Sour Meat Balls

150 3/4-inch (2 cm) balls

Great for a buffet.

4 pounds ground beef (2 kg)
 OR
2 pounds each, ground beef and ground veal (1 kg)

1/4 cup flour (60 mL)
1 1/2 teaspoons ground ginger (7 mL)
1 cup evaporated milk (250 mL)
1/4 cup soy sauce (60 mL)
4 tablespoons butter (60 mL)
1 1/4 cups ketchup (300 mL)
1/2 cup brown sugar (125 mL)
1/4 cup corn syrup (60 mL)
1/2 cup vinegar (125 mL)
2 cups water (500 mL)
2 tablespoons cornstarch (30 mL)

Mix the beef, flour and ginger in a large mixing bowl. Beat in the evaporated milk and soy sauce, 1 tablespoon (15 mL) at a time and beat until blended. Form the mixture into balls and fry in the butter until browned. Put the balls in a large casserole dish.

In a saucepan combine the ketchup, brown sugar, corn syrup, vinegar and water and bring the mixture to a boil. Mix the cornstarch with just enough water to form a paste. Add it to the sauce and boil again until thick and clear. Pour over the meat balls. Bake covered in a slow oven (275°F-140°C) for 2 hours.

Chili

A hit year-round but this is really our "skiing chili." I saw one of the friends we ski with picking out all the kidney beans the first time I brought chili. I brought the following chili next time and he cleaned his plate.

14 ounce can pork and beans (398 mL)
2 slices bacon
1 cup chopped onion (250 mL)
1 clove garlic, minced
1 1/2 pounds lean ground beef (750 g)
1 1/2 tablespoons chili powder (22 mL)
1/4 teaspoon thyme (1 mL)
1 teaspoon salt (5 mL)
1 tablespoon Worcestershire sauce (15 mL)
1 cup finely diced pear (canned or fresh) (250 mL)
2 19-ounce cans stewed tomatoes, coarsely chopped (2 540 mL)

Remove the pork from the pork and beans. Cut the bacon into small pieces and sauté it. Sauté the chopped onion and garlic in bacon fat until just limp. Add the ground beef and cook until all the pink disappears. Sprinkle chili powder over and blend in. Add all remaining ingredients and simmer, stirring occasionaliy for 1 hour.

Serve with a good crusty Italian or Portuguese loaf and a tossed green salad.

Liver with Onions and Bacon

Some people *like* liver—they really do! Find three liver-starved friends, whip up some mashed potatoes and put some French-cut green beans in a pot and have a feast in *very* short order.

1 pound calf liver (450 g)
4 or 5 slices bacon
3 tablespoons flour, seasoned with pepper and paprika to taste (45 mL)
10 ounce can condensed onion soup (284 mL)
4 tablespoons chili sauce (60 mL)
no salt

If the liver is not sliced when you buy it, slice it thinly. Cook the bacon until crisp and set aside. Pour off half the drippings. Dip the liver slices in the flour and cook them in the bacon fat just enough to brown each side lightly—no more than 2 to 3 minutes as liver usually comes sliced fairly thinly and has a tendency to be tough and dry when it is overcooked.

Combine the undiluted soup with the chili sauce in a small bowl. Tear the bacon into 1 inch (2.5 cm) pieces and add it to the sauce, then pour the sauce over the liver. Cover the pan and simmer over low heat for 5 minutes. Remove the cover and simmer for an additional 5 minutes, just long enough to thicken the sauce a bit.

Well-dressed Ham Slice
Serves 4

You can make the sauce in the morning then go off to the golf course to see if that "duck hook" you suddenly developed the day before is still there. Pour the sauce over the ham just before baking.

1 1 inch thick ham steak (2.5 cm)
whole cloves
3 tablespoons butter (45 mL)
3 tablespoons flour (45 mL)
10 ounce can consommé (284 mL)
3/4 cup orange juice (175 mL)
1/2 cup golden raisins (125 mL)
1/2 cup coarsely chopped water chestnuts (125 mL)
1/4 teaspoon ground cloves (1 mL)

With scissors, snip the fat edge of the ham in several places to keep it from curling, then stud the fat with a few whole cloves.

Melt 1 tablespoon (15 mL) of the butter and stir in the flour. Gradually add the consommé and orange juice. Add the raisins, water chestnuts and ground cloves. Stir over medium heat until slightly thickened. Remove from the heat and stir in the remaining 2 tablespoons (30 mL) of butter. Pour the sauce over the ham steak and bake covered in a 325°F (160°C) oven for 1 hour.

For an attractive meal, serve with asparagus, beets and baked sweet potatoes.

Note: To store water chestnuts in the refrigerator, place them in a jar and cover them with water. Replace the water with fresh water every day or so.

Poor Man's Beef Wellington

Serves 8

I may have misnamed this—ground beef isn't the bargain it used to be. But the dish is still a hit!

To round out your meal, serve French peas, Stuffed Tomatoes and a tossed green salad.

1 loaf of French bread
2 pounds lean ground beef (1 kg)
2 tablespoons horseradish (30 mL)
2 teaspoons salt (10 mL)
1 teaspoon dry mustard (5 mL)
1/4 cup milk (60 mL)
1/4 cup ketchup (60 mL)
3/4 cup onion, chopped (175 mL)
2 eggs, beaten
2 cups bread crumbs (500 mL)

Cut off both ends of the French bread and save them. Hollow the loaf, taking care not to break the crust. Use the soft interior to make bread crumbs for the meat filling.

To make the meat filling, combine all the remaining ingredients. Make sure they are well mixed.

To make the Wellington, stuff the meat mixture into the French loaf. Replace the ends. Wrap the loaf in foil and bake in a 350°F (180°C) oven for 1 hour. Then, open the foil, but do not remove it. Bake the loaf for an additional 10 minutes to crisp the crust.

To serve, slide the loaf onto a long platter and cut slices with a serrated knife. Pass Horseradish Sauce (page 51) or the following Mushroom Sauce separately.

Mushroom Sauce
1/2 pound fresh mushrooms (225 g)
3 tablespoons butter (45 mL)
4 teaspoons flour (20 mL)
1 1/2 teaspoons soy sauce (7 mL)
1 cup light cream (250 mL)
salt and pepper

Slice the mushrooms lengthwise. Melt the butter in a skillet and add the mushrooms. Sprinkle the flour over the mushrooms and toss the mushrooms until they are well coated. Cook over medium heat until the mushrooms are tender, stirring occasionally. Add the soy sauce, then slowly stir in the cream. Continue cooking, stirring constantly until the mixture bubbles and thickens. Season with salt and pepper. Serve hot.

Pork Chops in Mustard Cream
Serves 4

To hurry this dish along, eliminate the sautéed vegetables and serve a tossed salad with lots of cherry tomatoes.

3 to 4 tablespoons butter (45 mL to 60 mL)
1 bunch green onions, sliced
1 sweet red pepper, thinly sliced
4 ounces fresh mushrooms, sliced (125 g)
4 pork chops, trimmed to taste
1 cup heavy cream (250 mL)
2 tablespoons Dijon mustard (30 mL)
salt and freshly ground pepper to taste

Melt the butter in a skillet.* Add the green onions, red pepper and mushrooms and sauté until the vegetables are limp. Remove to a heated platter — ring the platter with the vegetables so the pork chops and sauce will fit in the center.

Sauté the pork chops lightly on both sides. Pour the cream over the chops and stir in the mustard (as best you can — it will slowly assimilate). Simmer until the sauce is reduced and coffee-colored and the chops are fork tender. Season with salt and freshly ground pepper. Place in the center of the ring of sautéed vegetables.

Serve with creamy mashed potatoes or buttered noodles.

* Don't use a skillet too large, as the heavy cream should almost cover the chops when you start simmering.

"Cordon Bleu" Meat Loaf

Serves 10

I had a request from a young friend to "please put your recipe for meat loaf in the next book." This is easier said than done as I don't really have a recipe. Like homemade soup, it can be different every time. Here is the last one I made — thoroughly enjoyed by the family. I am waiting for a call from Joy saying, "That's not the one I meant!"

2 pounds ground chuck (1 kg)
1 medium onion, finely chopped
1 carrot, grated
1 rib of celery, grated
1 1/3 cups fine cracker crumbs (325 mL)
2 eggs
1/2 cup milk (125 mL)
1 teaspoon dry mustard (5 mL)
2 tablespoons horseradish (30 mL)
1 teaspoon salt (5 mL)
6 slices cooked ham
8 slices Swiss cheese
5 hard-cooked eggs
4 strips bacon, cut in half

Combine all the ingredients *except* the ham, cheese, hard-cooked eggs and bacon. After mixing well, pat out on a piece of Saran wrap to make a rectangle 15 by 12 inches (37 cm × 30 cm). Place the ham slices on top of this, then lay out the cheese slices on top of the ham. Place the hard-cooked eggs in a row down the center.

Roll the loaf lengthwise. You want to encase the eggs in the middle. The Saran wrap will help you roll, as well as transfer this loaf, seam side down, to your baking pan. Remove the Saran. Make sure you seal the ends of the loaf well. Place the bacon strips over the top of the loaf. Bake in a 350°F (180°C) oven for 1 hour.

Serve hot with baked potatoes, Honey'd Onions and peas and mushroom sauce — serve cold with soft buns and crudités.

Mock Steak

Serves 4

Perfect for friends of relatives who chew Freedent gum! It's also a handy meal to prepare after a golf game, when "hurry up" is the order of the day.

1 1/2 tablespoons soy sauce (22 mL)
1 1/2 tablespoons Kitchen Bouquet for meat and gravy (22 mL)
1 pound ground round steak (or very lean ground chuck) (450 g)

Combine the soya sauce and Kitchen Bouquet in a small dish. Divide the meat into 4 portions and shape into patties or "thick hamburgers." Brush both sides of the patties with the combined liquids. Panfry or broil on both sides until medium-rare.

Don't overcook—it's not as nice. The flavor is fantastic. You need no salt or seasonings when you shape the meat—the liquid you brush on does it all. A baked potato and a salad are the only accompaniments you'll need.

Simple Veal Chops

Serves 2 to 4

Be sure to buy nice loin chops as the shoulder chops can be tough.

4 veal chops
garlic salt
1/2 cup dry vermouth (125 mL)
2 teaspoons Dijon mustard (10 mL)
1 to 2 teaspoons instant-blending flour (5 mL to 10 mL)

Sprinkle chops with garlic salt and brown them quickly in a mixture of butter and oil. Remove the chops to a casserole dish. Remove any excess fat from the pan and return it to the heat. Add the vermouth and bring it to a boil, stirring to loosen brown bits on the bottom. Stir in the Dijon mustard and a bit of instant-blending flour to thicken the sauce slightly. Pour this sauce over the chops and bake covered in a 325°F (160°C) oven for 1 hour or until tender.

Serve with boiled macaroni, well buttered and sprinkled with Parmesan cheese, French-style green beans and a sliced tomato salad.

Alberta-style Baked Pork Chops

Serves 3 to 4

Try these with Onion Casserole (page 119) and Niblets corn.

4 loin chops, 1 inch thick (2.5 cm)
1 egg, beaten
1 cup finely crushed potato chips* (250 mL)
2 tablespoons oil (30 mL)
10 ounce can condensed tomato soup (284 mL)
1/2 cup brown sugar (125 mL)
1 tablespoon vinegar (15 mL)
1/8 teaspoon nutmeg (0.5 mL)

Trim the fat from the chops, then dip them into the egg, then into the potato chips. Heat the oil in a skillet and brown the chops on both sides. Transfer them to a flat baking dish.

Combine the soup, sugar, vinegar and nutmeg and pour this mixture over the chops. Bake the chops in a 350°F (180°C) oven for 1 hour.

* A good way to crush potato chips is to put them in a plastic bag and roll a rolling pin over them.

Rolled Roast Loin of Pork

Serves 6 to 10

The combination of garlic and caraway seeds and roast of pork is indescribably good. When judging the amount of pork to buy, allow 1/2 pound (225 g) per person. There is quite a bit of shrinkage.

6 or 7 cloves garlic, minced
1 1/2 tablespoons caraway seeds (22 mL)
1 1/2 tablespoons salt (22 mL)
3 to 5 pounds rolled loin of pork (1.5 kg to 2.25 kg)
Spiced Peaches (optional)

Rub the garlic, caraway seeds and salt together to make a paste. Rub all over the roast. Bake in a 450°F (230°C) oven for 10 minutes. Reduce the heat to 325°F (160°C) and continue roasting for 25 to 30 minutes per pound (450 g) or until the meat thermometer registers 180°F (80°C).

Spiced Peaches
1 medium-sized can peach halves
1/2 cup packed brown sugar (125 mL)
1/3 cup vinegar (75 mL)
1 tablespoon grated orange rind (15 mL)
1 teaspoon whole cloves (5 mL)
1/2 teaspoon whole allspice (2 mL)

Drain the syrup from the peaches and combine 2/3 cup (150 mL) of the syrup with the remaining ingredients. Heat to boiling and simmer for 5 minutes. Add the peach halves and heat slowly for 5 minutes longer. Allow the peaches to stand for several hours or overnight in the liquid before serving. Drain and arrange around the platter of roast pork.

Serve with roast potatoes and broccoli with cheese sauce.

Danish Pork Tenderloin Serves 6

Nice with wild rice, French-cut green beans and broiled tomatoes.

2 pounds pork tenderloin (1 kg)
4 tablespoons butter (60 mL)
1/2 teaspoon salt (2 mL)
1/8 teaspoon cayenne (0.5 mL)
1/2 cup dry vermouth (125 mL)
1 tablespoon cornstarch (15 mL)
1 cup cereal cream (250 mL)
2 cups grated Dofino cheese (500 mL)

Cut the meat crosswise into serving portions, about 2 inches (5 cm) each in length. In a skillet brown the meat on both sides. Add the salt, cayenne and vermouth. Cover and simmer slowly for about 20 minutes, which should be sufficient time to cook it. Remove the meat to a warm platter, cover and keep warm.

Mix the cornstarch with the cream and add this mixture to the skillet. Simmer, stirring constantly until it starts to thicken. Stir in the cheese and heat just until it melts. Pour the sauce over the tenderloin and serve at once.

Pork Tenderloin "Liden" Serves 4

2 tablespoons butter (30 mL)
2 3/4-pound pork tenderloins, cut in half lengthwise (2 350 g)
1/4 cup hot water (60 mL)
1 cup bread crumbs (250 mL)
1 small onion, minced
1/2 cup raisins (125 mL)
1 tablespoon chopped parsley (15 mL)
salt and pepper to taste
1 cup chicken or beef bouillon (250 mL)
3/4 cup red wine (175 mL)

Melt the butter in a skillet and brown the meat on all sides. Remove the meat to a small roasting pan. Pour the hot water in the skillet and let it boil to catch all the drippings and brown bits.

Mix the bread crumbs with the onions, raisins, parsley and salt and pepper. Spread this mixture on the meat and sprinkle the hot water that you boiled in the skillet over the meat and crumbs. Add the bouillon, again sprinkling some on top of the crumbs.

Cover and bake in a 350°F (180°C) oven for 50 minutes. Uncover and sprinkle wine over all. Turn the oven up to 400°F (200°C) to allow the crumbs to brown and bake an additional 10 minutes, adding a bit more water at this time if it seems to be drying out.

Serve with mashed potatoes, baked acorn squash and a spinach salad.

Lynn's Stuffed Pork Tenderloin   Serves 6

For Pork Wellington — see the Note below.

1/3 cup butter (75 mL)
1 cup sliced mushrooms (250 mL)
1 medium onion, chopped
2 stalks celery, chopped
1 clove garlic, minced
thyme, summer savory, basil, salt and pepper to taste
3 cups soft bread crumbs (750 mL)
4 1/2-pound pork tenderloins (4 225 g)
1/4 pound bacon (110 g)

Melt the butter in a skillet and sauté the mushrooms, onions, celery and garlic until the onions are soft. Add thyme, summer savory, basil, salt and pepper to taste. Mix in the bread crumbs. If mixture does not hold together when you squeeze a handful, add a little more melted butter.

Split the pork tenderloins lengthwise so that they lie flat but are still in 1 piece. Place 2 of these in bottom of baking dish. Place the stuffing mixture on top, molding it a bit so it holds its shape pretty well. Place the remaining 2 tenderloins over the stuffing, so as to enclose it. You want round slices when you carve this. Tie the whole securely with string in several places. Cover the top with bacon strips. Bake in a 350°F (180°C) oven for 30 to 45 minutes per pound (450 g).

Note: To turn this into an elegant make-ahead entrée, prepare the above recipe the day before (omitting the bacon) and when cool, store in the refrigerator. The next morning, remove the string and wrap the tenderloin in thin slices of cooked ham and then in puff pastry (use the frozen dough). Place it back in the refrigerator until dinner. Bake in a 425°F (220°C) oven for 30 minutes or until the pastry is well browned.

Serve with Zucchini, Carrot and Green Onion Stir-fry and Wild Rice Casserole. A Caesar or a spinach salad are good accompaniments as well.

Easy Skillet Sausage Supper   Serves 3 to 4

The caraway seeds really make this dish for me.

2 medium onions
2 medium potatoes
1 pound pork sausages (450 g)
1 teaspoon caraway (or celery) seeds (5 mL)
1/2 teaspoon salt (2 mL)
1/4 teaspoon pepper (1 mL)
paprika to taste
2/3 cup water (150 mL)

Slice the onions thinly and separate them into rings. Peel the potatoes
and slice them in 1/4 inch (7 mm) slices.

Lightly oil a skillet and sauté the sausages until brown, but not cooked.
Drain off half the fat and add the onions. Sauté along with the sausages
until the onions are limp. Sprinkle caraway seeds on top. Lay slices of
potato on top. Sprinkle with salt, pepper and paprika. Add the water,
cover tightly and cook for about 20 minutes—or until the potatoes are
cooked.

ULTRA EASY — MEAT

Pitted prunes stuffed with sharp Cheddar cheese then wrapped in bacon and broiled make an interesting and tasty accompaniment to grilled pork chops, lamb chops or liver.

To make a flavorful stuffing for cabbage rolls or green peppers, combine 1/3 cup (75 mL) of applesauce with 1 pound (450 g) of ground beef.

To turn a vegetable casserole into a supper dish, split wieners or sausages lengthwise, spread them with Dijon mustard or horseradish and place them on the top of the casserole to bake with the vegetables.

Try grated raw potato in your next meat loaf instead of bread crumbs or cracker crumbs. The meat will have a lovely, moist texture. Use about 1/2 cup (125 mL) of grated potato for each 1 1/2 pounds (600 g) of meat.

The next time you cook a whole ham, don't discard the rind. Cut the rind into strips about 3 by 1/4 inches (8 cm × 7 mm), place the strips on a cookie sheet and bake them along with the ham until thoroughly rendered and crispy. They will curl up and turn into very tasty tidbits (they sometimes never make it out of my kitchen). As with peanuts, once you start, you can't stop.

My friend Doreen always rubs leg of lamb with curry powder before she roasts it. I swear I can't detect the curry flavor but the lamb is *outstanding*.

The Eighth Hole: Poultry and Game

Easy Baked Chicken   Serves 4

Late tee time? Not to worry — with recipes this simple (and tasty), you can even invite friends back with you.

2 1/2 to 3 pounds cut-up chicken (about 1.25 kg)
2 tablespoons butter or margarine (30 mL)
1 package dry onion soup mix

Place the chicken pieces in a baking dish. Dot with butter. Sprinkle with the dry onion soup mix. Bake *covered* in a 350°F (180°C) oven for 1 hour. There will be some juice in the bottom of the pan — delicious served over some hot fluffy rice.

Note: If you don't want to bother cooking the rice after you get home (I am not a great fan of minute rice) sprinkle 1 cup (250 mL) of long grain rice in the casserole before you add the chicken and onion soup, then pour a 10 ounce (284 mL) can of cream of mushroom soup mixed with 1 cup (250 mL) water and 2 tablespoons (30 mL) of chopped parsley over top. Bake covered at 300°F (150°C) for 2 hours. (You can do everything up to the baking before you leave for the course. Add an extra 20 minutes baking time if it comes straight out of the refrigerator.)

Chicken and/or Crab Crêpes   Serves 4 to 6

I thought crêpes were on their way out — but with the introduction of frozen crêpes on the supermarket scene, there has been a definite rekindling of interest. What does that tell you? It tells *me* that there are a lot of busy people out there who like crêpes, but don't have time for the time-consuming part — which is making the pancakes.

3 tablespoons minced green onions (45 mL)
2 tablespoons butter (30 mL)
5 tablespoons dry sherry (75 mL)
8 ounces cream cheese, softened (250 g)
1/4 cup milk (60 mL)
salt and pepper to taste
1 cup diced, cooked chicken (250 mL)
1 cup fresh or *well-drained canned* crabmeat (250 mL)
6 8 inch crêpes (20 cm)
3 to 4 tablespoons heavy cream (45 mL to 60 mL)

Sauté the green onions in the butter until soft. Add 2 tablespoons (30 mL) of the sherry and simmer for 2 to 3 minutes. Set aside.

Combine the cream cheese, milk and remaining 3 tablespoons (45 mL) of sherry and beat until smooth. Add the sautéed green onions and salt and pepper. (This will give you 1 1/2 cups — 375 mL of sauce). Add 1/2 cup (125 mL) of this sauce to the chicken and in a separate bowl add another 1/2 cup (125 mL) of the sauce to the crabmeat.

Lay the crêpes out on a counter and spoon about 1 tablespoon (15 mL) of the chicken mixture at one end of the crêpe and 1 tablespoon (15 mL) of the crab mixture at the other end. Roll up and place seam side down in a shallow buttered baking dish Thin out the re maining 1/2 cup (125 mL) of sauce with the heavy cream and spoon this over the top of the crêpes. (These can be refrigerated at this point.)

Bake in a preheated 325°F (160°C) oven for 15 to 20 minutes — 20 to 25 minutes if they have come from the refrigerator.

These crêpes and a tossed green salad or fresh fruit salad make a lovely luncheon.

Apricot Breast of Chicken
Serves 6 to 8

6 whole chicken breasts
1/2 cup melted butter (125 mL)
cornflake crumbs
12 tablespoons apricot brandy (180 mL)

Skin and bone the chicken breasts—you will now have 12 half breasts. Dip each piece in melted butter then coat it with cornflake crumbs. Place the breasts in a baking dish and tuck the ends in so the chicken breasts resemble little mounds. Bake in a 350°F (180°C) oven for 40 minutes. Remove from the oven and spoon 1 tablespoon (15 mL) of apricot brandy over each half breast.

Serve with wild rice (or the Uncle Ben's combination Long Grain and Wild Rice mix), some green beans and the Sweet Potato and Apricot Casserole on page 126.

Chicken with Chopped Almonds
Serves 6

4 boned, whole chicken breasts
1 cup raw almonds, coarsely chopped (250 mL)
2 tablespoons butter (30 mL)
1/2 cup white wine (125 mL)
Cream Sauce

Fry the chicken and 1/2 cup (125 mL) of the almonds in the butter until brown. Put the chicken and almonds in a casserole and pour the wine over them. Let sit while you make the cream sauce.

Cream Sauce
2 tablespoons butter (30 mL)
2 tablespoons flour (30 mL)
1 cup milk (250 mL)
salt and pepper to taste

Melt the butter over low heat. Add the flour and blend over low heat for 3 minutes. Gradually stir in the milk. Cook over medium heat until thickened and is smooth and hot. Salt and pepper to taste.

Pour the cream sauce over the top of the chicken and sprinkle with the remaining 1/2 cup (125 mL) of almonds. Bake in a 350°F (180°C) oven for 30 minutes.

Serve with baked potatoes, spinach and mushrooms.

Jay's Chicken Breasts

Serves 6

These can be prepared early in the day. Sharon's Pilaf (page 122) and a crisp salad are easy last-minute accompaniments.

6 whole chicken breasts, boned
flour
6 ounces plain yogurt (175 mL)
1/4 teaspoon basil (1 mL)
1/4 teaspoon thyme (1 mL)
1 tablespoon grated onion (15 mL)
juice of 1 lemon
dash of salt and pepper
1 cup cracker crumbs (250 mL)
1/2 cup grated Cheddar cheese (125 mL)

Dust the chicken with flour. Mix the yogurt, basil, thyme, grated onion, lemon juice and salt and pepper. Mix the cracker crumbs and cheese. Dip the chicken in the yogurt mixture, then in the cracker crumbs and cheese.

Place the chicken in a well-greased pan, tucking in the edges of the chicken to make mounds. Cover with foil and bake in a 350°F (180°C) oven for 30 minutes. Uncover and bake an additional 30 minutes.

Note: If you prepare this dish early in the day, do *not* cover it until you are ready to bake.

Cranberried Chicken

Serves 6 to 8

Super-easy recipes circulate very quickly, especially around a golf club where spare time in the kitchen is at a premium. I don't know where this recipe originated, but it came to me via Lola — via Millie!

1 can cranberry sauce
8 ounce bottle Russian salad dressing (250 mL)
1 package dried onion soup mix
5 to 6 pounds packages cut-up chicken (2.2 kg to 2.7 kg)

Combine the cranberry sauce, Russian dressing and onion soup mix. Coat the chicken with this mixture on both sides and bake covered in a 350°F (180°C) oven for 1 1/2 to 1 3/4 hours. Uncover for the last 15 minutes of cooking time.

Lemon-ginger Chicken Breasts

Serves 4 to 6

Simple, excellent and offered by my brother David, who is a terrific cook.

2 lemons
1 inch piece of raw ginger, grated (2.5 cm)
3 whole chicken breasts, boned, skinned and cut into 1 inch (2.5 cm)
   strips
2 tablespoons cooking oil (30 mL)
1 to 2 tablespoons butter (15 mL to 30 mL)
1 small can red pimientos, drained and diced

Combine the juice of 2 lemons, the grated rind of 1 lemon, the ginger and the oil. Place the chicken breasts in this marinade and let sit for about 2 hours. (If this is a golf day, do this in the morning and let it sit in the refrigerator until you're ready to cook.)

Sauté everything except the pimiento in the butter for roughly 3 to 5 minutes, or until cooked through. Sprinkle the pimiento over the chicken for the last minute or two of cooking and serve the chicken with the pan juices.

Chicken Marengo

Serves 4 to 6

See the "hurry up" version at the bottom!

3 pounds chicken parts (1.5 kg)
onion powder
garlic powder
paprika
1/2 teaspoon salt (2 mL)
3 tablespoons olive oil (45 mL)
1 can small whole white onions, drained
1/2 pound fresh mushrooms, sliced (225 g)
3 large tomatoes, chopped
2 tablespoons chopped fresh parsley (30 mL)
1 cup dry vermouth (250 mL)
2 tablespoons flour (30 mL)
1 can ripe black olives, drained

Sprinkle the chicken pieces with the onion powder, garlic powder, paprika and salt. Heat the olive oil in a skillet and sauté the chicken until golden brown on both sides. Remove the chicken to a large heated casserole dish. Arrange the white onions on top.

Add the mushrooms, tomatoes and parsley to the skillet and sauté for 2 minutes. Add the vermouth and cook until slightly reduced. Blend the flour with a bit of cold water and add it to the sauce. Cook and stir until thickened. Pour the sauce over the chicken. Bake *covered* in a preheated 325°F (160°C) oven for 1 hour. Remove the cover, add the black olives, return to oven just long enough for olives to be heated through.

Serve with hot buttered noodles and a green vegetable.

Note: Golfer's best friend? Canned soup! A "hurry up" version of this dish can be made by eliminating the fresh mushrooms, chopped tomatoes, vermouth and flour and substituting drained canned sliced mushrooms stirred into 2 10-ounce (284 mL) cans condensed golden mushroom soup and a 10 ounce (284 mL) can condensed tomato bisque. Pour this over the sautéed chicken pieces. Cover and bake as above.

Marinated Chicken

Serves 4

For an oriental touch, serve the marinated frying chicken with Chinese long-life noodles and stir-fried asparagus. (To cook dry Chinese noodles, simply add them slowly to rapidly boiling water, separate them with a fork and cook until *barely tender* — 4 to 6 minutes.)

2 1/2 to 3 pounds cut-up frying chicken (about 1.25 kg)
juice of 2 lemons
1/2 cup soy sauce (125 mL)
1/2 cup honey (125 mL)
1/2 cup tomato sauce or ketchup (125 mL)
2 tablespoons white wine (30 mL)
freshly ground black pepper
2 slices fresh ginger (optional)

Make a marinade by combining all the ingredients *except* the chicken, then marinate the chicken all day or overnight. (A plastic bag is good for this.) Remove the chicken from the marinade and bake in a 400°F (200°C) oven for 1 to 1 1/4 hours, basting with the marinade.

For 2 pounds (1 kg) of great barbecued chicken wings: Using above marinade as a key, delete the honey, tomato sauce and wine and marinate the wings in the soy sauce and lemon juice all day (remove the tips first). Drain and combine 1 tablespoon (30 mL) of the marinade with the honey, tomato sauce and pepper. Place the wings on the barbecue for 10 minutes, turn, baste with the honey mixture and cook for an additional 10 minutes. Repeat until the wings are cooked. (These may be done under the broiler as well.)

Pecan Chicken with Sherry Sauce

Serves 3 to 4

---

3 whole chicken breasts, skinned, boned and halved
salt and pepper
2 egg whites, beaten
1 cup finely chopped pecans (250 mL)

Sauce
2 tablespoons butter (30 mL)
2 tablespoons flour (30 mL)
1/2 cup chicken bouillon (125 mL)
1/2 cup cream (125 mL)
1/4 teaspoon salt (1 mL)
pinch of white pepper
1/4 cup grated Swiss cheese (60 mL)
2 tablespoons sherry (60 mL)
chopped parsley (garnish)
crisp bacon curls (garnish)

Season the chicken pieces with salt and pepper and dip them in the egg whites, then roll them in the chopped pecans. Place in a buttered baking dish and bake in a 350°F (180°C) oven for 20 to 25 minutes or until the chicken is cooked. Place in a heated platter and pour the sauce over.

To make the sauce, melt the butter and stir in the flour. Gradually add the chicken bouillon and cream. Add the salt and pepper. Cook stirring constantly until the mixture has thickened. Add the cheese and stir until just melted. Remove from the heat and stir in the sherry. Pour the sauce over the cooked chicken. Garnish with chopped parsley and crisp bacon curls.

Wild rice or brown rice, a green vegetable and broiled tomatoes are good accompaniments.

Favorite Way to Roast Whole Chicken

Serves 6 to 7

There *is* something between a fryer chicken and a turkey — it's called a roasting chicken. At one time these were very plentiful, now we have to search them out. I find mine at the Farmer's Market and like them around 5 to 6 pounds.

5 to 6 pound roasting chicken (2.5 kg)
butter or margarine
1/2 cup flour (125 mL)
1 teaspoon basil (5 mL)
1 teaspoon salt (5 mL)
1/4 teaspoon pepper (1 mL)
paprika

Wash and dry the chicken well. Stuff with the stuffing of your choice. (See Ultra Easy — Poultry.) Tie the feet together and tie the wings to the body. Smear the chicken well with butter or margarine. Combine the dry ingredients and shake the chicken with them in a paper bag. Remove the chicken from the bag and place it in a roasting pan. Sprinkle well with paprika. Bake for 1 hour in a 325°F (160°C) oven, then start basting every 10 to 15 minutes with the pan juices for an additional hour or until cooked.

Note: If you don't like stuffing and trussing a chicken or turkey, this casserole makes a good accompaniment. Nice with duck as well.

Mary Brown's Casserole Stuffing
1 package wild rice and long grain rice mix
1 pound fresh mushrooms (450 g)
1 pound sausage meat (450 g)

Prepare the rice according to the directions on the package. Cut the mushrooms into large-sized pieces and mix them into the rice. Mix in the sausage meat. Bake in a casserole dish (loaf shape) for 45 minutes in a 350°F (180°C) oven.

Roberta's Chicken

Serves 4 to 6

Roberta is not a golfer but her son John is and he thinks his mom's chicken is the greatest! (For "special" dinners, Roberta bones the chicken, but this dish is pretty special without that extra touch.)

1 cup white wine (250 mL)
1 teaspoon salt (5 mL)
1/4 teaspoon pepper (1 mL)
1/4 teaspoon rosemary (1 mL)
1/4 teaspoon summer savory (1 mL)
2 cloves garlic, finely minced

4 pounds cut-up frying chicken (2 kg)
4 tablespoons olive oil or butter (60 mL)
4 ounces ground almonds (125 g)
1/2 cup fine bread crumbs (125 mL)
1/2 teaspoon salt (2 mL)
1/4 teaspoon paprika (1 mL)
1 cup seedless grapes (250 mL)

Combine the first 6 ingredients and let the chicken marinate in this mixture for a minimum of 2 hours — no more than overnight. Turn occasionally.

Grease a baking dish well with *some* of the olive oil. Combine the ground almonds with the bread crumbs, salt and paprika. Roll each piece of chicken in this mixture, coating well. Reserve the marinade. Place the chicken in the greased baking pan and drizzle it with the remaining olive oil. Bake uncovered in a 350°F (180°C) oven for 45 minutes. Pour the reserved marinade over the chicken, add the grapes to the pan and bake an additional 5 minutes. If the chicken is not brown enough, place it under the broiler for 2 minutes.

Serve with fresh asparagus, George's Mushrooms and Sharon's Pilaf.

Sharon's French Chicken

Serves 4

Excellent — it really makes its own sauce. You can add mushrooms, small onions or the like, but it is delightful as is. If you have any leftovers, bone the chicken and make truly perfect sandwiches with crisp romaine and Russian dressing. Spoon the cold sauce — which will be an aspic — on the sandwiches, too.

2 or 3 slices bacon
3 pound cut-up frying chicken (the larger the better) (1.25 kg)
2 garlic cloves
generous handful of chopped parsley
paprika
salt
white pepper
2 to 3 ounces warmed brandy for flaming (50 mL to 75 mL)
1/4 cup white wine or chicken stock (60 mL)

Cook the bacon in a large skillet until crisp, crumble and set aside. Sauté the chicken in the bacon drippings until it is a nice golden color (it's not necessary to brown it). Sprinkle the chicken with the minced garlic, parsley, paprika, salt and pepper. Add the warmed brandy and flame. This much I do well in advance, then I clean up the mess.

When you're ready to cook, add a little white wine or chicken stock to the skillet, but not too much. Cover and simmer until tender — about 25 to 35 minutes. Serve with the crumbled bacon over the top.

Sweet and Sour Chicken

Serves 4

This is the easiest chicken dish I know to serve to a large crowd. Thank you Mrs. Pocklington from London, Ontario!

2 1/2 to 3 pounds cut-up chicken (1.25 kg)
1/4 cup soy sauce (60 mL)
1/2 cup bottled Chinese Sweet and Sour sauce (125 mL)
Chinese Brushes (garnish)

Marinate the chicken in the soy sauce for a few hours or overnight, turning once halfway through the marinating. Remove the meat from the soy sauce and place it in a buttered oblong baking dish. Bake in a preheated 350°F (180°C) oven for 30 minutes. Spoon the Sweet and Sour sauce over the top of the chicken and bake for an additional 30 to 40 minutes. Garnish with Chinese Brushes.

Chinese Brushes
Remove the tough green leaves from green onions (spring onions) and shred the tender green ends finely without removing the white part. Let the onions stand in ice water. The ends will curl up very attractively. This makes a nice garnish for any sweet and sour dish, not only for its decorative appeal — it also enhances the flavor of the dish.

Chicken with Orange Rind   Serves 4

2 1/2 to 3 pounds cut-up chicken (1.25 kg)
1 teaspoon salt (5 mL)
1/4 teaspoon pepper (1 mL)
1/4 teaspoon paprika (1 mL)
3 tablespoons butter or margarine (45 mL)
2 tablespoons slivered orange rind (30 mL)
2 tablespoons sugar (30 mL)
1/4 teaspoon ground ginger (1 mL)
1 cup orange juice (250 mL)

Sprinkle the pieces of chicken with the salt, pepper and paprika. Sauté the chicken in the butter (or margarine) until lightly browned on both sides. Remove the chicken and arrange it in a single layer in a shallow baking dish. Drain the fat from the skillet.

Remove rind from an orange with a vegetable parer, sliver and measure 2 tablespoons (30 mL). Put the orange rind in a small saucepan and cover it with boiling water. Simmer for 3 minutes. Drain.

Combine the sugar, ginger and orange juice in the skillet. Cook until the sugar is dissolved. Add the orange rind and pour this sauce over the chicken. Bake in a 350°F (180°C) oven for 1 hour.

Serve with rice, Stuffed Acorn Squash and a green vegetable.

Duck au Poivre

Serves 6 to 8

I use an electric coffee bean grinder to grind the pepper (it is just too tedious by hand). A blender would do the job as well but don't let it get too fine — you want a medium grind. And you *must* use freshly ground pepper but don't worry — it won't taste too peppery. The pepper takes on an almost nutlike flavor after it has been roasted. Absolutely delicious and very easy to prepare!

2 4 to 5 pound ducklings (2 2 kg)
garlic salt
3 oranges
3 cloves garlic
oil to rub over the duck
3 to 4 ounces freshly ground black pepper (75g to 100g)

Rinse the ducks inside and out and pat them dry. Sprinkle garlic salt *inside* each duck. Place 1 1/2 oranges, cut in quarters, and 1 1/2 cloves of garlic in the cavity of each duck. Close the openings with skewers or sew them shut. Rub the ducks with oil and let them sit in the refrigerator for a few hours.

Cover the ducks on all sides with the pepper — as heavy a coat as possible. Roast in a 325°F (160°C) oven for 3 hours and 30 minutes, pricking the skin frequently during the roasting period.

Remove the oranges and garlic and serve the ducks cut in quarters — game shears are perfect for this. Don't try to carve the ducks for it is better to leave as much of the skin intact as possible. It will be crisp and wonderfully flavored.

Note: Creamy mashed potatoes complement this duck perfectly. If you are giving an extra-special dinner party, make a ring of mashed potatoes and fill the center with chestnut purée. (Simply buy whole, canned chestnuts packed in water, drain them and put them through a ricer — or grate them with a food processor — then add a bit of butter and sugar, fluff them with a fork and heat them in the oven.) Celery and Almond Casserole and Alison's Cumberland Sauce make this a memorable meal.

Stuffed Rock Cornish Game Hens

Serves 2

2 Cornish game hens
1 1/2 cups seasoned croutons (375 mL)
1 1/2 tablespoons melted butter (22 mL)
12 mandarin orange sections, chopped*

Preheat the oven to 350°F (180°C).

Make the stuffing by tossing together the croutons, the melted butter and chopped orange sections. Wipe the hens clean inside and out and fill the cavities with the stuffing. Skewer or sew shut the openings. Tie the legs together and tie the wings to the body. Bake for 1 1/2 hours, basting frequently with the following sauce.

Basting sauce
1/4 cup honey (60 mL)
1/4 cup orange juice (60 mL)
1 teaspoon grated orange rind (5 mL)
1/2 teaspoon ginger (2 mL)
2 tablespoons melted butter (30 mL)

Combine all ingredients and use to baste the hens.

Remove the strings on the hens and serve with wild rice and Carrots with Ginger-pecan Sauce.

* If you can't find fresh mandarin oranges, use canned. Drain them well, then soak them in a bit of orange juice. This greatly enhances their flavor. Drain them well again before you add them to the stuffing.

ULTRA EASY—POULTRY AND GAME

If you don't know about the J-Cloth "stuffing bag" you should. It's perfect for a large roasting chicken or small turkey (frying chickens are too small). Open a J-Cloth to a single thickness, wet it with water and squeeze it, then line the inside cavity of the bird with the damp cloth. Spoon your dressing into the lined cavity. Pull the ends of the cloth together and tie them, forming a bag. Close the cavity with a skewer. When the bird is cooked, it's a simple matter to remove the bag and empty the steaming stuffing into a warmed serving bowl. (Storing leftover stuffing inside a bird is dangerous and this method ensures that *all* the stuffing is removed.) Try it!

To make a poultry stuffing quickly, add 1 tablespoon (15 mL) of dried onion soup mix to 3 cups (750 mL) of bread crumbs. (This saves you from peeling and chopping an onion and celery stalks.) Add the same amount of melted butter as you normally would—about 1/4 cup (60 mL). Mix in your favorite poultry seasoning, sage for some, summer savory for others.

No string to tie the bird? Use dental floss—it's very strong and doesn't burn.

The next time you cook a goose, save any leftover skin. The next day, bake the skin in the oven until it is well rendered and very crispy. Put the crispy skin between slices of the very best bakery bread you can find, unbuttered, and enjoy one of my most favorite sandwiches in the whole world!

For wonderful fried chicken, add some instant chicken soup base to the flour you use to coat the chicken. Use 1 tablespoon (15 mL) of the soup base to 1 cup (250 mL) of flour. No need to add salt—the soup base is salty enough.

A crazy time-saver—mix 3 parts salt to 1 part pepper in a shaker and keep it handy when you cook.

For lovely and moist barbecued chicken, give the chicken a start in a microwave oven—about 8 to 10 minutes.

The Ninth Hole: Eggs and Cheese

Overnight Breakfast Casserole

Serves 8 to 10

Perfect for a Sunday brunch party — or Christmas breakfast. Some warm muffins and a fresh fruit plate round out the offering.

6 slices bacon
1/2 pound cubed, cooked ham (225 g)
1/2 cup butter (125 mL)
1/2 cup flour (125 mL)
4 cups milk (1 L)
1/8 teaspoon salt (0.5 mL)
1/8 teaspoon pepper (0.5 mL)
16 eggs
1 cup evaporated milk (250 mL)
1/4 teaspoon salt (1 mL)
paprika

Sauté the bacon, break it into pieces and return it to the pan. Remove half the bacon fat. To the bacon bits and remaining fat, add the cubed ham and 1/4 cup (60 mL) of the butter. Sauté briefly.

Sprinkle the meat with the flour and stir well. Gradually add the milk and cook, stirring constantly until thickened. Season with the salt and pepper. Set aside while you prepare the eggs.

Beat the eggs into the evaporated milk. Add 1/4 teaspoon (1 mL) salt. Melt the remaining 1/4 cup (60 mL) of butter in a large skillet. Add the egg mixture and scramble until firm.

In a buttered 10 inch oven-proof casserole, put half the scrambled eggs and cover with half the cream-meat sauce. Add the remaining scrambled eggs and cover with remaining sauce. Place in refrigerator overnight.

In the morning bake in a 275°F (140°C) oven for 1 hour. Sprinkle the top with paprika.

Swedish Pancakes

Serves 2

These are not like pancakes *or* crêpes. Try them with syrup or sliced strawberries — just the thing for Sunday breakfast.

3 eggs
1 cup milk (250 mL)
4 tablespoons flour (60 mL)
1/2 teaspoon salt (2 mL)
1 tablespoon melted butter (15 mL)

Beat the eggs until light. Combine the milk, flour and salt and mix until smooth. Add this mixture to the eggs along with the melted butter.

Fry in a moderately hot frying pan in a mixture of butter and a bit of oil. Make your pancakes any manageable diameter but keep them as thin as possible.

Whole Wheat Pancakes or Breakfast Crêpes

Serves 4

Offer a variety of fillings with these and let your guests have the fun of assembling their own crêpes. Try bowls of chopped seasonal fresh fruit, sour cream, cottage cheese, blueberry conserve — whatever sounds good to you!

3 eggs
2 cups milk (500 mL)
2 tablespoons brown sugar (30 mL)
2 teaspoons vanilla (10 mL)
1 1/2 cups whole wheat flour (375 mL)
1 tablespoon melted margarine (15 mL)

Combine all the ingredients and let sit overnight. Whisk the batter and fry pancakes, using a fairly high heat. Serve hot.

Crustless Crab Quiche

Serves 6 to 8

This crustless quiche is perfect for the golfing season. Who has time to make pastry?

1 cup thinly sliced mushrooms (250 mL)
1 small onion, finely chopped
2 tablespoons butter or margarine (30 mL)
4 large eggs
1 cup 2% cottage cheese (250 mL)
1 cup sour cream (250 mL)
4 tablespoons flour (60 mL)
1/2 cup grated Parmesan cheese (125 mL)
1/4 teaspoon salt (1 mL)
1 cup grated Cheddar cheese (250 mL)
6 ounce can crabmeat, drained (175 g)

Sauté the mushrooms and onions in butter until tender. Set aside.

In a blender or food processor add all the other ingredients except the Cheddar cheese and crabmeat. Blend until thoroughly mixed. Pour this mixture into a mixing bowl and fold in the Cheddar cheese, crabmeat and sautéed vegetables. (Save the intact claw bits to decorate the top in a pinwheel design.)

Pour the mixture into a quiche dish or a deep buttered pie plate. Bake in a 350°F (180°C) oven for 45 minutes or until set (a knife inserted in the middle should come out clean).

Let sit for 10 minutes before serving. Serve with sliced beefsteak tomatoes, a tossed green salad and croissants for an easy luncheon.

Tomato and Avocado Quiche   Serves 6 to 8

2 tablespoons butter (30 mL)
1/3 cup chopped green onion (75 mL)
2 medium tomatoes
flour to dredge 1 sliced tomato
9 inch *deep dish* pastry-lined quiche dish or pie plate (1.5 L)
1/8 teaspoon oregano (0.5 mL)
1 cup grated Swiss or Monterey Jack cheese (250 mL)
4 large eggs
2 cups cereal cream (500 mL)
1/2 teaspoon salt (2 mL)
freshly ground black pepper to taste
1 small avocado

Melt 1 tablespoon (15 mL) of the butter and sauté the green onions until soft. Remove them from the pan and set aside.

Slice 1 tomato — there should be 6 or 7 slices. Add the remaining 1 tablespoon (30 mL) of butter to the pan. Dredge the slices in flour and sauté them very slightly. Arrange the tomato slices and sautéed onions on bottom of the pie crust. Sprinkle them with the oregano and the grated cheese.

Beat the eggs with the cream, salt and pepper until well blended but not frothy. Pour this mixture over the tomatoes, onions and cheese. Slice the remaining tomato thinly and arrange the slices on top of the quiche. Peel the avocado and slice it lengthwise. Arrange the avocado slices between slices of tomato — turning each once in the egg mixture to seal the surfaces from the air.

Bake in a 375°F (190°C) oven for about 40 minutes or until a knife inserted in the middle comes out clean.

Let sit for 10 minutes before serving. Serve with a spinach salad and pumpernickel rolls.

Scotch Eggs

14 pieces

A nice supper dish and a very popular "drink go along" at a cocktail party or backyard barbecue. Simple to make.

7 small hard-cooked eggs
flour (for dredging)
1 pound seasoned sausage meat (450 g)
1 egg, slightly beaten
bread crumbs
chopped parsley

Shell the eggs and chill them. Roll the cold eggs in a little flour. Press the sausage meat around the eggs, covering each completely. Dip each egg in the slightly beaten egg and roll it in bread crumbs.

Preheat deep fat to 375°F (190°C) and fry the eggs for 3 to 4 minutes, or until golden brown. Cut each egg in half and sprinkle it with chopped parsley.

Serve hot or cold.

Note: If you don't like to deep-fat fry, these can be baked in the oven. Bake for 10 minutes in a 400°F (200°C) oven, turn over and bake for an additional 10 minutes.

Sunday Morning Eggs

Serves 4

6 ounces canned crabmeat, drained (175 g)
4 fresh artichoke bottoms, cooked
    OR
8 canned artichoke bottoms
4 poached eggs
Hollandaise Sauce (page 50)

Place the crabmeat on top of the artichoke bottoms and place in a very slow oven on individual plates to warm while you poach the eggs. Place a poached egg on top of each artichoke bottom with crabmeat. (If you use the canned artichokes, use 2 per person and arrange one on either side of the poached egg.) Coat all with Hollandaise Sauce.

Welsh Rarebit

Serves 6

For a twist, omit the almonds in the recipe below and place pieces of cooked bacon and sautéed fresh mushrooms over toast points before adding the Welsh Rarebit.

1 tablespoon butter (15 mL)
1 cup beer (250 mL)
1 teaspoon dry mustard (5 mL)
2 1/2 teaspoons Worcestershire sauce (12 mL)
dash of cayenne
dash of paprika
1/4 teaspoon salt (1 mL)
1 pound Cheddar cheese, shredded (450 g)
2 eggs
whole toasted almonds (garnish)

Melt the butter in the top of a double boiler. Combine the beer, mustard, Worcestershire sauce, cayenne, paprika and salt and add this mixture to the butter. Have the water in the double boiler simmering, not boiling, and add the cheese to the beer mixture 1/4 at a time and stir until melted. Beat the eggs in a small bowl and gradually stir in a little of the cheese mixture, enough to warm the eggs. Stir all back into the top of the double boiler and cook, stirring constantly until the mixture thickens. This will take about 5 minutes.

Serve over toast points and sprinkle with a few whole toasted almonds.

The Tenth Hole: Vegetables

Asparagus (or Broccoli) with Sour Cream Sauce
Serves 4

You can cook the asparagus in the morning and prepare the sauce and buttered crumbs. Just before serving, heat the sauce, pour it over the asparagus, sprinkle it with crumbs and place the whole under broiler.

1/2 cup sour cream (125 mL)
3 tablespoons mayonnaise (45 mL)
1 tablespoon lemon juice (15 mL)
1 1/2 pounds fresh asparagus (or broccoli), cooked tender-crisp* (700 g)
1/4 cup buttered dry bread crumbs (60 mL)

Combine the sour cream, mayonnaise and lemon juice. Pour this over the asparagus (or broccoli), top with buttered crumbs and place the whole under the broiler until the sauce is bubbly and the crumbs are golden brown.

* See Ultra Easy — Vegetables for the best way to cook asparagus.

Beets with Orange Sauce
Serves 6 to 8

1 tablespoon butter (15 mL)
1 1/2 tablespoons flour (22 mL)
4 tablespoons brown sugar (60 mL)
1 cup orange juice (250 mL)
3 cups diced, cooked fresh or canned beets (750 mL)
1/8 teaspoon salt (0.5 mL)
pinch of white pepper

Melt the butter in a small saucepan. Combine the flour and sugar and add this mixture to the butter along with the orange juice. Cook, stirring until thickened. Add the beets, salt and pepper.
  Serve hot.

Savory Broccoli Bake

Serves 10

People often ask me, "Can you really play a round of golf the same day you are entertaining 20 people at dinner?" The answer is yes. It is not that difficult when you plan ahead and have recipes like this one (doubled*) which takes so little time to put together. It can be baked ahead and reheated when the roast (or whatever) comes out, if you are cramped for oven space.

2 10-ounce cans condensed potato soup (2 284 mL)
1/2 soup can of milk
1/2 cup Miracle Whip (*not* mayonnaise) (125 mL)
2 pounds chopped frozen broccoli (1 kg)
1 cup grated Cheddar cheese (250 mL)

Combine the potato soup, milk and Miracle Whip. Fold in the broccoli and pour into a buttered casserole dish. Sprinkle grated cheese on top and bake in a 350°F (180°C) oven for 1 hour.

* If you double the recipe, increase the baking time to 1 1/2 hours.

Individual Broccoli Soufflés

Serves 8

1 pound fresh broccoli (450 g)
1/2 cup heavy cream (125 mL)
juice of 1/2 lemon
1/2 teaspoon salt (2 mL)
pinch of nutmeg
pinch of black pepper
4 eggs

Cook the broccoli for 10 minutes. Drain and rinse under cold water and set aside.

In a small saucepan combine the cream, lemon juice, salt, nutmeg and pepper. Boil for 10 minutes by which time the cream will almost have disappeared. Scrape this mixture into a blender or food processor. Add the broccoli and purée. Beat the eggs well and add them to the purée. Combine well.

Fill buttered timbale molds, individual casseroles or medium-sized muffin tins. Set them in a pan of water and bake in a preheated 375°F (190°C) oven for about 30 minutes or until firm.

Unmold and serve.

Broccoli Stir-fry

Serves 10 to 12

Last minute tasks are to be avoided when you're entertaining, but you can still serve this stir-fry at a dinner party. Prepare as directed but *undercook* the broccoli. Reheat it in the microwave just before serving. (You can't go wrong if you *undercook* — overcooked broccoli is a disaster.)

2 pounds fresh broccoli (1 kg)
6 tablespoons oil (90 mL)
1 clove garlic, finely minced
salt and pepper
1 cup water (250 mL)

Separate the broccoli into flowerets. Pare the stems and slice them diagonally.

Heat the oil, garlic, salt and pepper in a frying pan. Add the broccoli to the pan and sauté over fairly high heat for about 2 minutes, stirring constantly. Add the water, cover the pan tightly and cook the broccoli for an additional 5 minutes or until cooked but still a bit crisp.

Note: For very bright green broccoli, plunge the broccoli spears into rapidly boiling water to which has been added 1 tablespoon (15 mL) of baking soda. Remove and drain immediately.

Carrot and Turnip Purée

Serves 6

This can be made ahead and reheated. Your guests will think it is squash (which would be costlier) but will soon discover the difference when they taste the wonderful flavor that blending these two vegetables produces.

1 1/2 pounds carrots (700 g)
1 1/2 pounds turnips (700 g)
2 tablespoons butter (30 mL)
salt and pepper to taste

Cook the carrots and turnip together in boiling salted water until tender. Purée the vegetables through a food mill or in a food processor. Add the butter, salt and pepper. Stir until the butter has melted.

Creamed Cabbage

Serves 6 to 8

This is particularly good with pork or game.

1/4 cup minced onion (60 mL)
2 tablespoons butter (30 mL)
4 cups shredded cabbage (1 L)
4 ounces cream cheese (125 g)
1 teaspoon dried dill (or to taste) (5 mL)
salt and white pepper to taste

Sauté the minced onion in the butter until it is soft. Set aside.

Cook the shredded cabbage in 2 cups (500 mL) boiling water until *just* tender. (I sometimes add 2 teaspoons (10 mL) of instant chicken soup mix to the water, but this is not necessary.) Drain the cabbage, return it to the pot and while still hot, add the cream cheese in small pieces and the sautéed onion. Stir until the cheese has melted. You may have to return this to the heat for a minute or two to get the cheese completely melted. Stir in the dill and salt and pepper to taste.

Carrots with Ginger-pecan Sauce

Serves 6

Frozen carrots are quick, but need a little dressing up. These are dressed up so nicely, you could serve them at your most elegant dinner party. Nice with chicken or pork — and you can make the sauce ahead of time.

1 tablespoon brown sugar (15 mL)
2 tablespoons lemon juice (30 mL)
2 tablespoons butter (30 mL)
2 tablespoons finely chopped green onion (30 mL)
2 tablespoons sliced pecans (30 mL)
1/8 teaspoon ground ginger (0.5 mL)
1/8 teaspoon pepper (0.5 mL)
1/4 teaspoon salt (1 mL)
1 pound frozen small whole carrots (450 g)

In a small saucepan dissolve the sugar in the lemon juice. Add all the remaining ingredients *except* the carrots. Heat until the butter has melted and the sauce is heated through.

Cook the carrots according to the directions on the package and drain well. Pour the sauce over the drained hot carrots.

Baked Whole Cauliflower with Cheese Sauce

Serves 4 to 6

A very attractive and easy way to serve cauliflower—even more smashing surrounded by lightly sautéed cherry tomatoes and snow pea pods.

1 medium cauliflower
10 ounce can Cheddar cheese soup (284 mL)
1/2 cup grated sharp Cheddar cheese (125 mL)
toasted whole almonds

Steam the cauliflower until it is crisp-tender.

Heat the Cheddar cheese soup. Add the grated cheese and stir until the cheese is melted. Pour this sauce over the partially cooked cauliflower and bake in a 350°F (180°C) oven for 25 minutes. Remove the cauliflower from the oven and decorate with toasted almonds. Stick the almonds all over the cauliflower so that it resembles a porcupine!

Note: If you have any of this dish left over, chop the cauliflower (fairly fine), add 1 beaten egg and enough bread crumbs to bind. Shape this into patties and fry on both sides until golden. (Your family will never know it's leftovers!)

Honey'd Onions

Serves 6 to 8

So good with roast beef or roast pork.

6 large onions
2 tablespoons butter (30 mL)
2 tablespoons honey (30 mL)
2 tablespoons lemon juice (30 mL)
1/2 teaspoon salt (2 mL)
1/4 teaspoon pepper (1 mL)
paprika

Peel the onions and cut them in half crosswise. Place them in a buttered shallow baking dish. Melt the butter and add the honey, lemon juice, salt and pepper. Heat until all the ingredients are well blended, then pour this sauce over the onions. Sprinkle the top with paprika.

Bake in a preheated 350°F (180°C) oven for 1 hour. Turn once or twice during the baking time.

Celery and Almond Stir-fry   Serves 6 to 8

Celery is often overlooked in menu planning, but its unique flavor complements many a fish and game dish — also poultry. For a small dinner (under 8) I like to use the stir-fry version, often substituting a can of sliced water chestnuts for the almonds. For a large dinner party, I use the casserole version below, as this can be assembled in the morning or even the night before. The larger the party — the more you do ahead!

4 cups thinly sliced celery (1 L)
3 tablespoons butter (45 mL)
8 green onions (including most of the green part) sliced
2 cloves garlic, minced
1 cup blanched almonds (250 mL)
 OR
1 can sliced water chestnuts, drained
salt and pepper to taste

Pour boiling water over the sliced celery then let the celery sit while you prepare the remaining ingredients. Melt the butter in a large fry pan over medium heat. Add the green onions, garlic and almonds (or water chestnuts). Sauté for 2 minutes, stirring frequently. Add the drained celery, increase the heat to medium-high and stir-fry for an additional 4 to 5 minutes. You want the celery to retain a certain amount of crispness. Season with salt and pepper.

Casserole Make-Ahead Method   (Serves 8)
4 cups sliced celery (1 L)
1 cup old Cheddar cheese, grated (250 mL)
10 ounce can condensed cream of chicken soup (284 mL)
10 ounce can condensed cream of celery soup (284 mL)
1 cup blanched almonds (250 mL)
buttered cracker crumbs (garnish)

Cook and drain the celery. Mix the celery with the cheese, soups and almonds. Place the mixture in a buttered casserole dish. Sprinkle the buttered crumbs on top and bake in a 350°F (180°C) oven for 45 minutes.
    (When doubling, do not double the soup: use 1 can cream of chicken and 2 cans cream of celery.)

Corn Soufflé

Serves 10 to 12

This does not rise a great deal like most soufflés, but then unlike most soufflés, this can be completely assembled and oven-ready the night before!

6 large eggs
2 14-ounce cans cream-style corn (2 398 mL)
1 small onion, finely chopped
3/4 teaspoon salt (3 mL)
1/8 teaspoon white pepper (0.5 mL)
1/8 teaspoon cayenne (0.5 mL)
4 to 5 tablespoons chopped fresh parsley (60 mL to 75 mL)
2/3 cup *white* bread crumbs, no crusts (150 mL)
2/3 cup grated Cheddar cheese (150 mL)
2/3 cup heavy cream (150 mL)

Beat the eggs then add all the remaining ingredients. Empty this mixture into a buttered soufflé dish (8 cup — 2 L). Cover and refrigerate all day or overnight.

Before baking, place the dish in hot water — about 1/2 inch (1.5 cm) of water (you want the water to come about two-thirds of the way up the side of the dish). Bake in a preheated 350°F (180°C) oven for 30 minutes. Reduce the heat to 325°F (160°C) and continue baking for 1 1/4 to 1 1/2 hours. Let rest for 10 minutes with the oven door ajar before serving.

Glazed Cucumbers

Serves 4 to 6

It is often difficult to decide on just the right vegetable to serve with fish — you don't want to overpower the delicate flavor of the fish. This cucumber dish is perfect.

2 large cucumbers
1/4 cup butter (unsalted if you have it) (60 mL)
2 tablespoons lemon juice (30 mL)
   OR
1 tablespoon each of lemon juice and chicken stock (15 mL)
salt to taste
1/2 teaspoon sugar to sprinkle (2 mL)
1 tablespoon finely chopped parsley (15 mL)

Peel the cucumbers and cut them in half lengthwise. Scrape out the seeds with a spoon. Cut the cucumbers into sticks the size of your little finger. Heat the butter in a skillet, add the cucumbers, lemon juice and salt. Cover and let cook over moderately high heat, shaking the skillet back and forth frequently, for about 5 minutes or until the sticks are shiny and cooked but still firm. Remove the cover. Sprinkle the cucumbers with sugar and continue to cook them until they are a light golden color. Sprinkle with chopped fresh parsley.

Stuffed Eggplant

Serves 4 to 8

Perfect with lamb, but also good with beef or pork — and most of the work can be done ahead of time.

2 small eggplants
4 tablespoons oil (60 mL)
2 medium onions, chopped
1 clove garlic, minced
2 medium tomatoes, chopped
1 teaspoon oregano (5 mL)
1/4 pound mushrooms, sliced (110 g)
2 tablespoons tomato paste (30 mL)
1 cup grated mozzarella cheese (250 mL)
salt and pepper

Cut the eggplants in half and scoop out the inside (reserving the pulp). Leave a shell about 1/4 inch (7 mm) thick. (A grapefruit knife is good for this purpose.) Salt the insides of the shells and let them sit while you make the filling.

Pour the oil into a large skillet and sauté the onions and garlic. While the onion is cooking chop the eggplant pulp and add it to the onions, which should be soft at this stage, but not brown. Sauté until the eggplant starts to soften. Add the tomatoes and oregano. Cook, stirring frequently for about 10 minutes. Add the mushrooms and tomato paste and about 1/2 teaspoon (2 mL) of salt. Cook, stirring frequently for an additional 10 minutes. Check the seasoning. Remove from heat. Pour off any liquid that has accumulated in the salted shells and fill the shells with cooked mixture. (At this point the eggplants may be refrigerated.)

Sprinkle the tops of the eggplant halves with the mozzarella cheese and bake in a 350°F (180°C) oven for 35 to 45 minutes or until the shells are soft when pierced with a fork. Serves 1/4 to 1/2 eggplant per person.

Onion Casserole
Serves 4

Nice with steak, roast beef or pork.

4 medium onions, sliced thinly
3 tablespoons butter (45 mL)
2 tablespoons flour (30 mL)
1 cup beef bouillon (250 mL)
1 1/2 cups cheese and garlic croutons (375 mL)
1/4 cup grated Parmesan cheese (60 mL)

Sauté the onions in the butter until limp. Sprinkle them with the flour and blend. Gradually add the bouillon, stirring constantly until thickened and bubbly. Pour the mixture into a casserole dish. Sprinkle croutons on top. Sprinkle Parmesan cheese on top of the croutons. Bake in a 350°F (180°C) oven for 30 minutes.

Note: I quadrupled this recipe for a dinner party for 20 — very easy if you have a food processor to slice the onions. If you are making this for a large party, sauté the onions until limp and make the cream sauce separately. Pour the sauce over the onions and bake in a 325°F (160°C) oven for 1 hour. This can be assembled in the morning but don't add the croutons and cheese until you are ready to bake.

George's Mushrooms

Serves 4 to 6

1 pound whole mushrooms (450 g)
4 teaspoons sherry (20 mL)
garlic powder
2 tablespoons butter (30 mL)
1/2 cup chopped onion (125 mL)
1/4 cup chopped celery (60 mL)
1/4 cup chopped green pepper (60 mL)
salt and pepper to taste
4 slices cooked bacon
1/2 cup grated Swiss cheese (125 mL)

Separate the mushroom caps and stems and chop the stems. Arrange the mushroom caps in a buttered glass pie plate. Sprinkle them with 2 teaspoons (10 mL) of the sherry and a light sprinkling of garlic powder. Set aside.

Melt the butter and sauté the chopped mushroom stems, chopped onions, celery and green pepper, stirring frequently until the vegetables are almost tender but not brown. Stir in the remaining 2 teaspoons (10 mL) of sherry and the salt and pepper. Crumble the bacon and sprinkle it over the mushrooms in the pie plate. Spoon the vegetable mixture over the mushrooms and bacon. (If you are making this ahead of time, refrigerate at this point.)

Sprinkle the grated cheese on top of all and bake in a 350°F (180°C) oven for about 20 minutes or until the cheese is melted and the vegetables are heated through.

French Peas

Serves 4

I have tried "French Peas" (peas cooked with lettuce) several times and thought, "The French can have them!" Then I discovered the following method, which is to put the lettuce in just at the end. It makes all the difference — no more soggy discolored lettuce.

10 ounce package frozen peas (275 g)
1/2 teaspoon garlic salt (2 mL)
1/4 head of iceberg lettuce (head lettuce), shredded
2 tablespoons butter (30 mL)

Cook the peas according to the instructions on the package, using just slightly less water. Just before the peas are cooked, remove the cover and sprinkle them with the garlic salt and shredded lettuce. Continue cooking until the peas are done but still firm and the lettuce is soft. Drain and toss with butter.

Nut Loaf

Serves 6 to 8

There is a lady at our golf course—10 years my senior with 10 times my energy—who bounces down the 18th fairway while I am dragging my feet. One day I asked her, "What do you eat?" She replied, "I have a bowl of Red River Cereal every morning for breakfast." I bought a box on the way home thinking the family would enjoy it. They didn't. However, they had this Nut Loaf a few weeks later and thought it was just great. It goes very nicely with chicken.

2 cups uncooked Red River cereal (500 mL)
1 cup boiling water (250 mL)
1 cup cereal cream (250 mL)
1 small onion, finely chopped
1 cup walnuts, chopped (250 mL)
1/2 teaspoon oregano (2 mL)
1 teaspoon salt (5 mL)
2 eggs, beaten
1 cup grated Cheddar cheese (250 mL)

Pour the boiling water over the cereal, stir in the cream and let stand for 10 minutes. Stir in the remaining ingredients and place in a well-buttered loaf pan. Bake in a preheated 350°F (180°C) oven for 1 hour.
Serve hot in place of rice or potatoes.

Sharon's Armenian Pilaf

Serves 6

The Chinese are born knowing how to cook rice, and cooking pasta is second nature to the Italians. A friend in Escondido, California, cooks them together, a dish she learned while living in an Armenian community. It makes an interesting accompaniment to poultry or pork.

1/2 cup vermicelli, coarsely crumbled (125 mL)
melted butter
1 cup rice (250 mL)
2 cups water (500 mL)
a bit of granulated chicken bouillon

Cook the vermicelli in melted margarine until good and brown. Rinse the rice in water until the water runs clear. Boil 2 cups (500 mL) water. Add the rice and vermicelli to the boiling water. Do not add any salt to the water but add a bit of granulated chicken bouillon for extra flavoring. Stir to combine. Don't cover until the water disappears from the top of the mixture and bubbles form. When this happens, cover, turn to very low heat and "steam" for about 15 to 20 minutes. Let sit for 10 to 20 minutes before serving.

Note: This holds for quite a long time and can be reheated slowly.

Pilaf Stuffed Tomatoes
This is a nice way to use any leftover pilaf and it makes a very attractive vegetable.

Peel firm tomatoes and scoop out the centers. Salt the insides lightly, then turn upside down on paper towels to drain. Spoon pilaf into the shells. Bake in a 350°F (180°C) oven for 10 to 20 minutes — just long enough to reheat the pilaf. Sprinkle the tops with pine nuts if you have them.

Easy Potato Bake

Serves 4

I keep waiting for one of the children to detect the cottage cheese and complain about the little "lumps." This has gotten through without detection every time I have served it — with requests for seconds!

1 cup cream-style cottage cheese (2% is fine) (250 mL)
1/2 cup sour cream (125 mL)
2 tablespoons chopped green onion (30 mL)
1/8 teaspoon garlic powder (0.5 mL)
1/8 teaspoon pepper (0.5 mL)
3/4 teaspoon salt (3 mL)
2 1/2 cups diced cooked potatoes (625 mL)
1/2 cup shredded Cheddar cheese (125 mL)

Combine all the ingredients *except* the potatoes and Cheddar cheese. Stir this mixture into the potatoes and place in a casserole dish. Sprinkle the top with cheese. Bake in a 350°F (180°C) oven for 30 minutes.

Note: If you double or triple this recipe, increase the baking time — 45 minutes if you double, 1 hour if you triple or more.

Jane's Potato Casserole

Serves 6

Do you ever wonder what lady golfers talk about between shots? We exchange recipes, that's what! This tasty dish comes from someone in my "Thursday group."

4 to 5 medium potatoes
1 package *Heinz* dry onion soup mix
2 tablespoons butter (30 mL)
1 cup grated sharp Cheddar cheese (250 mL)

Peel the potatoes and cut them into 1 inch (2.5 cm) cubes. Place the potatoes in a buttered casserole, sprinkle with half the package of the onion soup mix, dot with butter, sprinkle with half the cheese. Repeat once more. Cover and bake in a 350°F (180°C) oven for 45 minutes. Remove the cover and continue to cook for an additional 15 minutes.

Potato Puffs

Serves 4 to 6

Don't try to prepare these for too many people (4 to 6 at the most) as they are a last minute vegetable which requires your undivided attention.

1 1/2 cups cream puff paste (625 mL)
1 1/2 cups mashed potatoes (625 mL)
oil for deep frying

Combine the cream puff paste (the packaged is fine) and the mashed potatoes. Heat the oil to 360°F (about 180°C). Fry small spoonfuls of the mixture, about the size of walnuts, in the deep fat until golden.

Note: These potatoes will puff up a good deal, so do not use too much batter for each puff.

Swiss Mashed Potatoes

Serves 8

With just a little extra trouble, plain mashed potatoes can be transformed into a gourmet dish!

6 cups mashed potatoes (1.5 L)
1/4 cup butter or margarine (60 mL)
3 tablespoons flour (45 mL)
2 cups milk, scalded (500 mL)
2 egg yolks
1 1/2 cups grated Swiss cheese (375 mL)
1 teaspoon salt (5 mL)
1/4 teaspoon nutmeg (1 mL)
1/8 teaspoon white pepper (0.5 mL)
2 tablespoons grated Swiss cheese (topping) (30 mL)

Spread the potatoes in the bottom of a 9 by 13 inch (3.5 L) baking pan and set aside.

Melt the butter in a medium saucepan. Blend in the flour and add the scalded milk slowly, stirring constantly. When this mixture thickens, remove it from the heat. Add the egg yolks carefully (adding a little of the hot mixture to the beaten egg yolks first). Stir until well blended. Add the 1 1/2 cups (375 mL) grated cheese, salt, nutmeg and pepper. Stir until the cheese melts.

Pour the sauce over the mashed potatoes and sprinkle with 2 table-spoons (30 mL) of Swiss cheese. Bake in a 375°F (190°C) oven for 20 minutes or until heated through, then place the pan under the broiler until the top is golden brown.

Dry Potatoes with Ginger and Garlic
Serves 4

This recipe originated with a Scottish girl living in Spain and came to me via a Nova Scotian girl living in Silver Lake, Ohio. I have since sent it to a friend in Switzerland. So you see, this recipe is all over the world! Cook the potatoes in the morning or the night before — then you are all set to go.

1 1/2 pounds potatoes (625 g)
2 tablespoons fresh ginger, peeled and chopped (30 mL)
3 cloves garlic, peeled
3 tablespoons water (45 mL)
1/2 teaspoon ground turmeric (2 mL)
1 teaspoon salt (5 mL)
1/4 teaspoon cayenne (1 mL)
5 tablespoons sunflower or peanut oil (75 mL)
1 teaspoon whole fennel seed (5 mL)

Boil the potatoes in their skins. Drain and cool the potatoes completely, then peel and dice them in 3/4 to 1 inch (2 cm to 2.5 cm) pieces. Put the ginger, garlic, water, turmeric, salt and cayenne in a blender and blend to form a paste. Heat the oil in a large frying pan over medium heat. When hot, add the fennel seed. Sizzle for a few seconds. Add the ginger-garlic paste and stir-fry for about 2 minutes. Add the potatoes and stir-fry for 5 to 7 minutes over medium-high heat or until the potatoes have a nice golden brown crust

Crisp-crusted Potatoes   Serves 4

Great with roast beef, roast lamb or roast pork. Vary the amounts to suit the number of people you are serving.

1/2 teaspoon salt (2 mL)
1 cup bread crumbs (250 mL)
4 medium potatoes, pared and cut in half crosswise
1/3 cup melted butter (75 mL)

Mix the salt with the bread crumbs. Dip the potato halves in the melted butter then roll them in the bread crumbs. Place the potatoes on a baking sheet. Spoon any leftover butter over the tops of the potatoes. Bake in a 350°F (180°C) oven for about 1 hour, or until tender when pierced with a fork. Turn the potatoes halfway through the cooking time.

Sweet Potato and Apricot Casserole
Serves 8

Nice with turkey and ham.

2 19-ounce cans sweet potatoes, sliced (2 540 mL)
14 ounce can apricot halves (398 mL)
1 cup brown sugar (250 mL)
1 1/2 tablespoons cornstarch (22 mL)
1/4 teaspoon salt (1 mL)
1/8 teaspoon cinnamon (0.5 mL)
1 teaspoon grated orange rind (5 mL)
2 tablespoons butter (30 mL)

Arrange the sweet potatoes in the bottom of a buttered casserole. Drain the apricots, save the juice and cut the apricot halves in half again. Arrange these on top of the sweet potatoes.

In a small saucepan combine the sugar, apricot juice, cornstarch, salt, cinnamon and orange rind. Bring this sauce to a boil and cook over medium heat for 2 minutes. Remove from the heat and stir in the butter. Pour the sauce over the sweet potatoes and apricots. Bake covered in a 350°F (180°C) oven for 30 minutes.

"Brown" Rice
Serves 4

Wonderful flavor.

1 large onion, chopped
2 tablespoons oil (30 mL)
1 cup long-grain rice (250 mL)
2 cups chicken or beef bouillon (500 mL)

Fry the onions in the oil until *very* brown, stirring frequently so they don't burn. Add the rice and fry until the rice is transparent. Add the bouillon. Cover and bring to a boil. As soon as the mixture comes to a boil, immediately turn the heat to simmer and cook over very low heat for 45 minutes. Do not remove the cover at any time.

Wild Rice Casserole
Serves 10 to 12

Nice with poultry or game.

2 cups wild rice (500 mL)
  OR
1 cup each of wild rice and brown rice (250 mL)
4 green onions, finely chopped
4 tablespoons chopped fresh parsley (60 mL)
1/4 cup butter (60 mL)
3 10-ounce cans consommé, undiluted (3 284 mL)
1/4 cup sherry (60 mL)
salt and pepper to taste

Cook the *wild* rice in a covered pot in boiling salted water for 5 minutes. Remove from the heat and let stand for about 1 hour. Drain and place in buttered casserole dish.

Sauté the onions and parsley in the butter until the onions are tender. (If you use brown rice, sauté it with the onions and parsley.) Add this to the wild rice. Heat the consommé and pour it over the rice. Stir in the sherry. Add a little salt and pepper. Bake covered in a preheated 350°F (180°C) oven for 50 to 60 minutes or until all the liquid is absorbed.

Note: This may be cooked the day before and reheated in a 350°F (180°C) oven for 30 minutes.

Creamed Spinach

Serves 4 to 6

Garnish this with 1 finely chopped hard-cooked egg when it comes out of the oven and serve it with seafood for a splendid simple meal.

about 24 ounces frozen chopped spinach (600 g)
4 ounces cream cheese (dice and leave at room temperature) (125 g)
2 tablespoons softened butter (30 mL)
1 1/2 teaspoons horseradish (7 mL)
dash of salt
dash of pepper

Cook the spinach and drain very well. Stir in the cream cheese, butter, horseradish, salt and pepper while the spinach is still hot. Place in buttered casserole dish. Bake in a 350°F (180°C) oven for about 20 minutes, or until hot and bubbly.

Stuffed Tomatoes

Serves 6 to 8

6 to 8 medium, firm tomatoes
1/2 cup butter (125 mL)
1 cup chopped onion (250 mL)
1 clove garlic, minced
1/2 teaspoon salt (2 mL)
1/4 teaspoon black pepper (1 mL)
1 teaspoon sugar (5 mL)
1/2 to 3/4 cup dry bread crumbs (125 mL to 175 mL)
6 ounce jar marinated artichoke hearts, drained (175 mL)

Wash and halve the tomatoes and carefully scoop out their insides, saving the pulp. You should have 12 to 16 hollow shells. Place them upside down on a double thickness of paper towels to drain.

Meanwhile, melt the butter, add the onions and garlic and cook until soft. Add the tomato pulp and cook for 5 minutes. Add the salt, pepper and sugar. Stir in enough bread crumbs to bind the mixture together. Cook until the crumbs absorb all the moisture. Chop the artichoke hearts coarsely and add them to the bread mixture. Fill the tomato shells with this mixture. Dot with a bit of butter and bake in a 375°F (190°C) oven for 15 to 20 minutes.

Stuffed Acorn Squash

Serves 8

The cranberry and apple filling makes this a lovely dish for Christmastime entertaining.

1/4 cup finely chopped onion (60 mL)
3 tablespoons butter (45 mL)
1 1/2 cups fresh cranberries (375 mL)
1 1/2 cups chopped, unpeeled apple (375 mL)
1 teaspoon lemon juice (5 mL)
2 tablespoons water (30 mL)
1/2 cup brown sugar (125 mL)
1/2 teaspoon salt (2 mL)
1/8 teaspoon pepper (0.5 mL)
4 small acorn squash

Sauté the onions in the butter for 2 minutes. Add the cranberries, apple, lemon juice, water, sugar, salt and pepper. Bring this mixture to a boil and simmer for 5 minutes. Set aside. (You can do this much in the morning.)

Cut the squash, clean them and place them cut side down in baking dish. Add water to a depth of 1/2 inch (1 cm). Bake for 45 minutes in a 375°F (190°C) oven. Remove the squash from the oven, turn right side up and fill with the cranberry mixture. Reduce the heat to 350°F (180°C) and bake for an additional 15 minutes or until the squash is soft when pierced with a fork.

Broiled Tomatoes

Serves 4 to 6

Bacon, tomatoes and green onion — always a good combination. Make the topping in the morning then halve the tomatoes, dress and broil them in the evening at serving time. Easy.

6 tomatoes
1/2 cup mayonnaise (125 mL)
1/2 cup crumbled, crisp bacon (125 mL)
1 1/2 tablespoons chopped green onion (22 mL)
1/4 teaspoon dried basil (1 mL)
freshly ground black pepper to taste

Cut the tomatoes in half. Combine the remaining ingredients and place a spoonful of this mixture on top of each tomato half. Broil until the tops are golden.

Tomatoes Rockefeller

Serves 12

My long-time friend Mary Maclean served these to her friend Beverly Sills when Beverly was visiting in Edmonton and was immediately asked for the recipe.

about 24 ounces frozen spinach, cooked, drained and chopped (600 g)
2 cups bread crumbs (500 mL)
3 green onions, white part only, chopped fine
6 eggs, beaten
1/2 cup melted butter (125 mL)
1/2 cup grated Parmesan cheese (125 mL)
1/2 teaspoon minced garlic (2 mL)
1/2 teaspoon thyme (2 mL)
1/4 teaspoon cayenne (1 mL)
1/2 teaspoon black pepper (2 mL)
6 large firm tomatoes, cut in 1/2 inch (1 cm) slices

Mix all the ingredients *except* the tomatoes. (This may be done ahead of time.)

Place the tomato slices on a greased cookie sheet. Place a mound of the spinach mixture on each tomato slice (an ice cream scoop is good for this). Bake in a 350°F (180°C) oven for 20 minutes.

Baked Cherry Tomatoes in Cream

Serves 4

Special—but don't make them for too large a group for they have to be peeled and it is a bit time-consuming. Pour boiling water over them for a few seconds so the skins will peel easily.

1 pint cherry tomatoes, peeled (500 mL)
2 tablespoons butter (30 mL)
1 tablespoon brown sugar (15 mL)
1/4 teaspoon salt (1 mL)
pinch of basil
1/4 cup heavy cream (60 mL)

In a small skillet, sauté the tomatoes in the butter until just warmed through. Sprinkle them with the sugar, salt and basil and cook for 1 minute, stirring constantly. Remove the tomatoes to a warmed serving dish. Pour the heavy cream into the juices remaining in skillet and boil it for just a minute or two. This will thicken a wee bit—then pour it over the tomatoes. Serve at once.

Green Tomato Casserole   Serves 8

Great with steak and a favorite vegetable dish at the Marks house. Pat is a fellow golfer who can literally hit the ball *out of sight*.

2 tablespoons butter (30 mL)
1 tablespoon oil (15 mL)
8 green tomatoes, sliced
3 large onions, sliced
1/2 teaspoon curry powder (2 mL)
salt and paprika to taste
1 cup sour cream (250 mL)
1/2 cup buttered bread crumbs (125 mL)
2 tablespoons grated Parmesan cheese (30 mL)

In a large skillet melt the butter, add the oil and cook the tomatoes and onions until they are soft. Stir in the curry powder, salt and paprika to taste. Let the mixture cool.

Gently stir in the sour cream. Pour all into a casserole dish. Mix the buttered crumbs and Parmesan and sprinkle this mixture over the tomatoes and sour cream. Bake in a 350°F (180°C) oven for 20 to 25 minutes or until the mixture bubbles and the crumbs are brown.

Turnip Puff

Serves 4

Our daughter Louise — who couldn't even be *bribed* to eat turnip (this usually worked with the other children) — decided, at age 13, that she wanted to help with Sunday dinner. I said, "Great, make the turnip puff." She made it, she ate it and she has been eating it ever since!

1 1/2 cups cooked mashed turnip (375 mL)
1 egg, well beaten
1 tablespoon butter (15 mL)
1 1/2 tablespoons flour (22 mL)
1 1/2 teaspoons brown sugar (7 mL)
1 teaspoon baking powder (5 mL)
1/4 teaspoon salt (1 mL)
dash of white pepper
3 tablespoons buttered crumbs (45 mL)

Combine the turnip and egg and beat well. Add all the remaining ingredients and mix until well blended. Turn into a well-buttered casserole and sprinkle with buttered crumbs. Bake in a preheated 375°F (190°C) oven for 20 to 25 minutes.

Zucchini, Tomato and Mushroom Casserole

Serves 6

1 pound zucchini, sliced (450 g)
1 pound tomatoes, sliced (450 g)
8 ounces fresh mushrooms, sautéed (225 g)
2 tablespoons Parmesan cheese (30 mL)
freshly ground black pepper to taste
1/2 cup heavy cream (125 mL)
1/2 cup buttered bread crumbs (125 mL)

Lightly sauté the zucchini. Arrange layers of zucchini, tomatoes and mushrooms. Sprinkle with Parmesan cheese and freshly ground black pepper. Pour the heavy cream over the vegetables. Top with buttered crumbs and bake in a 350°F (180°C) oven for 30 minutes.

Fruit Mélange

Nice with ham or pork.

28 ounce can peach halves or slices (800 mL)
28 ounce can pears (800 mL)
14 ounce can mandarin oranges (398 mL)
14 ounce can pineapple chunks (398 mL)
6 ounce jar maraschino cherries (175 mL)
1/2 cup golden raisins (125 mL)
3/4 cup brown sugar (175 mL)
1/4 cup butter (60 mL)
2 tablespoons lemon juice (30 mL)

Drain the fruit well and place it in an oven-proof oblong casserole
(13 by 9 inch — 3.5 L). Sprinkle the raisins on top, then sprinkle all
with the brown sugar. Dot with butter. Pour the lemon juice over all
and bake for 1 hour in a 350°F (180°C) oven. Refrigerate overnight.
On the next day, reheat for 30 minutes in a 350°F (180°C) oven.

Zucchini, Carrot and Green Onion Stir-fry

Serves 6

Very colorful. You can cut the vegetables ahead of time and cook them
just before serving or cook the entire dish an hour or two ahead and
place it in a microwave to reheat it. (Don't leave it in the microwave
a second longer than necessary as you only want to heat, *not cook*.)

2 medium zucchini
6 medium carrots
6 or 7 green onions
2 tablespoons oil (30 mL)
1 teaspoon salt (5 mL)

With a sharp knife cut the zucchini into 2 by 1/2 inch (5 cm × 1 cm)
sticks. Cut the carrots into a similar shape but a little thinner as they
require a longer cooking time. Cut the green onions into 1 inch (2.5
cm) pieces.

In a skillet or wok heat the oil and add the carrots and green onions.
Cook for 5 minutes, stirring frequently over fairly high heat. Add the
zucchini and salt and cook for an additional 3 minutes or until crisp-
tender, stirring frequently.

Baked Peach Halves

These add a decorative touch to baked ham or pork roast.

8 peach halves
8 teaspoons chutney (40 mL)
curry powder

Place 1 teaspoon (15 mL) of chutney in each peach half. Sprinkle with a bit of curry powder — just lightly. Bake in a 350°F (180°C) oven for 15 to 20 minutes.

Minted Pears

Lovely surrounding a platter of roast of lamb.

1 cup mint jelly (250 mL)
1/4 cup light corn syrup (60 mL)
1/4 cup white vinegar (60 mL)
20 ounce can pears (575 mL)
1 tablespoon crème de menthe (15 mL)

Combine the mint jelly, corn syrup and vinegar in saucepan and heat the mixture until the jelly melts. Add the pears and crème de menthe and simmer for 15 minutes. Chill and serve.

ULTRA EASY — VEGETABLES

Moisten any dry stuffing mix with a little melted butter and use it as a topping on broiled tomatoes.

Top hot cooked spinach with sour cream mixed with a bit of horseradish.

Parsley will stay fresh longer if you wash it and store it in a covered glass jar in the refrigerator. I don't know why, it just does.

Use hot beef bouillon over scalloped potatoes instead of cream or cream sauce. Potatoes are not fattening, it's what you put on them.

To keep sliced potatoes from turning brown, immerse them in a cold water-lemon juice solution — 3 cups (750 mL) of cold water to 2 table-spoons (30 mL) of lemon juice.

To keep pasta from boiling over, add a tablespoon (15 mL) of oil to the water.

Save your pickle juice to pour over canned beets for (what else?) pickled beets! Drain the beets before you pour in the pickle juice and store them in the refrigerator.

To make quick Duchess Potatoes, make 2 1/2 to 3 cups (675 mL to 750 mL) of instant mashed potatoes, using 2 tablespoons (30 mL) *less* liquid than called for. Beat in 1 egg and 1 egg yolk until the potatoes are nice and fluffy. Force the mixture through a pastry tube or spoon it around a plank or baking dish. Bake until lightly browned (about 5 minutes).

Need potatoes in a hurry? Keep a can of small white potatoes on hand for emergencies. Blend 3 tablespoons (45 mL) of butter and 2 1/2 tea-spoons (12 mL) of dry mustard in a saucepan. Add the drained pota-toes and roll them in the butter mixture. Let the potatoes simmer until they are a nice golden brown.

Cooking asparagus without a tall narrow pot can be cumbersome, but *baking* asparagus couldn't be easier. Break off the tough ends, peel the stalks with a vegetable peeler, enclose the asparagus in a sheet of foil and crumple the edges slightly to seal the package. Bake in a 425°F (220°C) oven for 20 to 30 minutes or until tender. I guarantee excel-lent results.

Refrigerate onions before you peel them to minimize tears.

Sprinkle potatoes lightly with flour before you fry them for a nice golden color.

When buying vegetables or salad greens, hold your hand over the bin to see that there is no warmth, i.e., fermentation. Packaged vegetables should not have steam bubbles inside the cellophane.

When fresh dill is in season, snip some onto a cookie sheet and freeze it. When frozen, transfer it to a small plastic container and store it in the freezer. Mix a bit of "fresh frozen" dill with the mayonnaise the next time you make cucumber sandwiches. Lovely.

For a twist, mix hot drained green beans with sour cream, a bit of grated raw onion and a squeeze of lemon.

For more substantial cream-style corn, add a can of drained regular canned corn to a can of cream-style.

Add fresh mint to the water when you are boiling potatoes to accompany any lamb dish.

The Eleventh Hole: Leftovers

Leftover Roast Beef Stir-fry

Serves 2

You can use this recipe with leftover poultry or pork as well.

1 1/2 tablespoons oil (22 mL)
1 clove garlic
1 small piece fresh ginger (optional)
1 cup roast beef, cut in thin strips, across the grain (250 mL)
1 stalk broccoli, diagonally sliced
1 stalk celery, diagonally sliced
2 green onions, cut in 1 inch (2.5 cm) pieces
1/2 green pepper, cut in narrow strips
1 tablespoon soy sauce (15 mL)
1 tablespoon water (15 mL)
1 teaspoon cornstarch (5 mL)

In a skillet heat the oil and cook the garlic and ginger for 2 minutes, then discard. Sauté the beef and vegetables, stirring until the vegetables are tender-crisp. Mix the soy sauce, water and cornstarch and add this to the meat and vegetables. Cook, stirring until thickened.
   Serve over rice.

Doreen's Roast Beef Blintzes

mashed potatoes
cooked leftover roast beef, ground
seasoned salt
pepper
fried chopped onions
crêpes
sour cream

The above amounts will depend on how much roast beef you have
left over.

Combine the mashed potatoes, beef, salt, pepper and fried onions.
Shape into cylinders and roll in crêpes — tucking in the ends as you roll.
Place in buttered baking dish and bake in a 350°F (180°C) oven until
heated through — about 20 minutes.

Serve 2 per person and top with sour cream.

Chicken Crêpes   Serves 2 to 4

If you have individual oven-proof dishes, use them for this. If you have
played 18 holes — you can probably eat 2!

4 large thin crêpes
1 cup thick white sauce (250 mL)
2 tablespoons sherry (30 mL)
2 cups cut-up cooked chicken (500 mL)
2 tablespoons finely minced green onion (30 mL)
1/2 cup chopped toasted almonds (125 mL)
2/3 cup mayonnaise (150 mL)
2 egg whites, stiffly beaten
4 tablespoons Parmesan cheese (60 mL)

Make (or buy) the crêpes and set aside. Mix together the white sauce,
sherry, chicken, onions and almonds. Divide this mixture between the
4 crêpes and roll them. Place the crêpes in a buttered baking dish.

Fold the mayonnaise gently into the egg whites and spread this mixture over the crêpes. Sprinkle the crêpes with the Parmesan. Bake in a
375°F (190°C) oven for 10 minutes.

Chicken or Turkey Casserole   Serves 4 to 6

Easy — excellent!

1 package long grain and wild rice mix
10 ounce can condensed cream of chicken soup (284 mL)
3/4 cup water (175 mL)
1/4 cup sherry (60 mL)
1 1/2 tablespoons soy sauce (22 mL)
3 cups cooked chicken or turkey, cubed (750 mL)
1/3 cup chopped green onion (75 mL)
10 ounce can water chestnuts, drained and quartered (284 mL)
1 small can chow mein noodles
   OR
1 cup buttered bread crumbs (250 mL)

Cook the rice and mix according to the directions on the package. Combine the soup, water, sherry and soy sauce. Mix in all the remaining ingredients, including the rice but *not* the chow mein noodles. Place the mixture in a casserole dish and sprinkle the noodles on top. Bake in a 350°F (180°C) oven for 45 minutes.

Chef's Chicken Salad   Serves 2

1 1/2 cups cooked chicken, cut in julienne strips (375 mL)
3 cups shredded lettuce (750 mL)
1/2 cup julienne strips of Swiss cheese (125 mL)
1 cup mayonnaise (250 mL)
1 tablespoon chopped green pepper (15 mL)
1 tablespoon chopped red pepper (15 mL)
1 tablespoon white wine vinegar (15 mL)
pinch of tarragon
2 tablespoons chili sauce (30 mL)
lettuce leaves
strips of cooked bacon (garnish)

Mix the chicken, shredded lettuce and cheese. Combine the mayonnaise, green peppers, red peppers, vinegar, tarragon and chili sauce and mix gently into the chicken-lettuce mixture. Place the whole in a bowl lined with lettuce leaves and garnish with strips of bacon.

"Another" Chicken Casserole   Serves 4

Even my husband, who is allergic to leftovers, likes this one!

2 cups cooked chicken (or turkey), cubed (500 mL)
2 hard-cooked eggs, sliced
1 1/2 cups dry herb-seasoned stuffing mix (375 mL)
1 tablespoon chopped parsley (15 mL)
salt and pepper
pinch of garlic powder
1 cup milk (250 mL)
2/3 cup Miracle Whip (150 mL)

Mix the chicken, eggs, 1/2 cup (125 mL) of the stuffing mix and the parsley. Place in a buttered 8 inch square (2 L) baking dish. Sprinkle with the salt, pepper and garlic powder.

Combine the milk and Miracle Whip and pour this over the chicken mixture. Top with the remaining 1 cup (250 mL) of stuffing cubes. Bake for 30 minutes in a 350°F (180°C) oven.

A fruit salad would be a nice accompaniment.

Curried Turkey (or Chicken) Salad
Serves 4

3 ounces slivered almonds (75 g)
2/3 cup mayonnaise (150 mL)
1 1/2 teaspoons curry powder (7 mL)
1 tablespoon Dijon mustard (15 mL)
1/8 teaspoon salt (0.5 mL)
3 cups cooked turkey (750 mL)
5 ounces water chestnuts (125 mL)
8 ounces seedless grapes (225 g)
1/2 cup sliced celery (125 mL)
Boston or Bibb lettuce

Toast the almonds on a well-buttered pan in a 350°F (180°C) oven until they are golden brown—about 10 minutes. Set aside to cool and sprinkle with salt.

Combine the mayonnaise, curry powder, Dijon mustard and salt. Let this sit in the refrigerator for about 1/2 hour to blend the flavors.

Combine the turkey, water chestnuts, grapes, celery and almonds and mix well with mayonnaise mixture. Serve on soft lettuce leaves.

Chicken Pie with Biscuit Topping

Serves 6

During the golfing season, you can use Tea Biscuit mix for the topping (not *quite* as good, but very presentable).

1/4 cup butter (60 mL)
1/4 cup flour (60 mL)
1 cup milk (250 mL)
1 cup chicken bouillon (250 mL)
1/4 teaspoon salt (1 mL)
pinch of white pepper
2 cups cut-up cooked chicken or turkey (500 mL)
1 cup cooked vegetables (carrots, celery or mushrooms) (250 mL)
1 cup frozen peas (250 mL)

Melt the butter in a small saucepan. Stir in the flour. Gradually add the milk and chicken bouillon, then add the salt and pepper. Cook, stirring constantly until the mixture starts to thicken. Add the meat, cooked vegetables and peas. Place in a shallow 13 by 7 inch (2.5 L) casserole dish.

Biscuit Topping
2 cups flour (500 mL)
4 teaspoons baking powder (20 mL)
1/2 teaspoon salt (2 mL)
1/3 cup cold butter (75 mL)
3/4 cup milk (175 mL)
1 cup grated cheese (optional) (250 mL)

Sift the flour, baking powder and salt into a bowl. Cut in the butter until you have pieces the size of peas. Pour milk into the center of the flour mixture and stir until the mixture comes away from the sides of the bowl. Knead gently on lightly floured surface for 1 minute. Roll out to 1/4 inch (7 mm) thickness. Sprinkle with the grated cheese. Roll as for a jelly roll and cut in 1/2 inch (1 cm) slices (about 12 pieces). Place the slices on top of the chicken and bake in a preheated 425°F (220°C) oven for 20 minutes.

Hot Chicken or Turkey Sandwiches

Serves 4

If you are asking yourself whether these are good enough to bother making the white sauce — the answer is yes!

White Sauce
2 tablespoons butter (30 mL)
2 tablespoons flour (30 mL)
1 1/2 cups milk (375 mL)
1/2 teaspoon salt (2 mL)
pinch of pepper
pinch of cayenne

4 slices French or Dutch bread, toasted
1 medium, mild onion, thinly sliced
8 slices cold chicken
   OR
4 slices cold turkey
2 tomatoes
4 slices Swiss cheese
1/4 cup Parmesan cheese (60 mL)
4 slices bacon, cooked and crumbled

To make the white sauce, melt the butter, stir in the flour and gradually add the milk. Cook, stirring until the mixture begins to thicken. Add the salt, pepper and cayenne. Set aside.

Place the toast in a buttered 8 inch square (2 L) baking dish. Separate the onions into rings and place them on the toast. Layer the chicken (or turkey), tomatoes and cheese slices on top of the onions, in that order.

Bake in a 325°F (160°C) oven until the cheese starts to melt — about 10 minutes. Remove from the oven and pour the white sauce over all. Sprinkle with the Parmesan and return to the oven for an additional 10 to 15 minutes.

Sprinkle with the bacon bits and serve hot.

Overnight Chicken (or Turkey) Casserole

Serves 6 to 8

8 slices day-old bread
2 cups cooked, diced chicken (or turkey) (500 mL)
1/2 cup mayonnaise (125 mL)
1 cup celery, chopped (250 mL)
1 small onion, finely chopped
2 ounce jar pimientos, drained and chopped (50 g)
1 cup sliced mushrooms (250 mL)
4 large eggs
3 cups milk (750 mL)
10 ounce can condensed cream of mushroom soup (284 mL)
1 cup grated Cheddar or Swiss cheese (250 mL)

Butter a 9 by 13 inch (3.5 L) shallow casserole dish. Remove the crusts from the bread and cut 4 of the slices into cubes. Arrange these cubes in the bottom of the casserole. Mix the chicken with the mayonnaise, celery, onions, pimientos and mushrooms and place this on top of the bread cubes. Lay the remaining 4 slices of bread on top. Beat the eggs slightly and mix them with the milk. Pour this mixture over the top of the mixture in the casserole dish and refrigerate overnight.

On the next day, place the casserole dish in a pan of hot water and bake the whole in a 350°F (180°C) oven for 20 minutes. Remove this from the oven and gently spread the mushroom soup over the top. Sprinkle with the grated cheese and return to the oven for 1 hour.

Serve hot. (Sprinkle the top with paprika if you've used Swiss cheese.)

Ham and Pineapple

Serves 2

4 slices canned pineapple, drained
2 tablespoons mayonnaise (30 mL)
1 teaspoon Dijon mustard (5 mL)
1 cup ground ham (250 mL)

Place pineapple slices in buttered casserole dish. Mix the mayonnaise with the mustard and stir this mixture into the ground ham. Divide the ham mixture equally among the pineapple slices, spreading it evenly on top of each slice. Bake in a 350°F (180°C) oven for 10 to 15 minutes, just until heated through.

Ham and Broccoli Casserole   Serves 4 to 6

You might find yourself buying ham on a more regular basis now that you have this quick and *delicious* way to use up the leftovers.

1 pound frozen French fries (450 g)
10 ounce package frozen chopped broccoli (275 g)
2 cups diced cooked ham (500 mL)
1/2 cup Miracle Whip (*not* mayonnaise) (125 mL)
3/4 cup milk (175 mL)
10 ounce can condensed cream of mushroom soup (284 mL)
1 cup shredded sharp Cheddar cheese (250 mL)

Butter a 13 by 9 inch (3.5 L) oblong baking dish. Place the French fries in the bottom (it doesn't matter if the fries or broccoli have thawed). Spread the broccoli over the potato layer. Spread the ham over the broccoli. Combine the Miracle Whip, milk and mushroom soup and pour this mixture over the top of the vegetables and ham. Bake in a preheated 350°F (180°C) oven for 20 minutes. Remove from the oven, sprinkle cheese over the top and return to the oven for an additional 20 minutes.

Ham Balls for Pea Soup   10 to 12 balls

Homemade pea soup needs no dressing up, but these will take the "ho-hum" out of canned or packaged pea soup.

1 cup ground cooked ham (250 mL)
1 egg, slightly beaten
1 tablespoon flour (15 mL)
1/2 teaspoon dry mustard (2 mL)
1/4 cup fine bread crumbs (60 mL)
salt and pepper to taste

Combine all the ingredients. If the mixture is too sticky, add a bit more bread crumbs. (Salt carefully as the amount you need will depend on the saltiness of the ham.) Form the mixture into small balls and *either* bake them in a 350°F (180°C) oven for 10 minutes *or* simmer them very gently in pea soup for about 3 minutes.

Curried Lamb

Serves 2 to 3

2 tablespoons butter (30 mL)
2 teaspoons curry powder (10 mL)
1/4 cup chopped onion (60 mL)
1/2 apple, peeled and chopped
1 1/2 tablespoons flour (22 mL)
3/4 cup chicken bouillon (175 mL)
2 tablespoons raisins (30 mL)
1 1/2 cups diced cooked lamb (375 mL)

Melt the butter and fry the curry powder in it for a minute or two. Add the onions and apples and sauté them until they are soft but not brown. Sprinkle the mixture with the flour and stir until the flour is absorbed. Stir in the bouillon and cook for a minute or two. Stir in the raisins and lamb and continue to cook until the mixture is slightly thickened.

Serve hot over rice.

Salmon Soufflé

Serves 4 to 6

When I bake a whole salmon, I often have lots left. I like it cold but the children don't, so I find this recipe very useful. This works well with canned salmon, too.

1/2 cup shredded cheese (or Cheez Whiz) (125 mL)
10 ounce can condensed cream of celery soup (284 mL)
3 eggs, separated
2 cups cold, flaked salmon (500 mL)
2 cups fresh bread cubes or crumbs (500 mL)
2 tablespoons grated onion (30 mL)
1 tablespoon chopped parsley (15 mL)

Heat the cheese and soup together over low heat until the cheese melts. Remove from the heat and cool. Beat the egg *yolks* and add them to the soup-cheese mixture. Stir in the salmon, bread cubes, grated onion and chopped parsley. Fold in 3 stiffly beaten egg whites. Put the mixture into a buttered soufflé dish. Place the dish in a pan of hot water and bake in a 350°F (180°C) oven for 40 minutes or until the center is set.

Nice with Cucumber Sauce.

Curried Roast Pork
Serves 4

If I have just a little cold pork left, I usually add it to a stir-fry, but if I have more, I like the following recipe. It's a snap.

1 1/2 tablespoons butter (22 mL)
1/2 cup chopped onion (125 mL)
1/2 cup fresh sliced mushrooms (125 mL)
1 ripe tomato, peeled and chopped
1 1/2 teaspoons curry powder (7 mL)
10 ounce can condensed golden mushroom soup (284 mL)
1/2 cup milk (125 mL)
1 1/2 to 2 cups cooked pork, cubed (375 mL to 500 mL)
1/4 teaspoon salt (1 mL)
1/2 to 1 cup sour cream (125 mL to 250 mL)
chopped fresh parsley (garnish)

Melt the butter and sauté the onions, mushrooms, tomato and curry powder until the onion is soft. Stir in the soup and milk and when smooth, add the pork and salt. Simmer for about 10 minutes. Stir in the sour cream, but do not allow to boil after the cream has been added, or it will curdle.

Serve over hot fluffy rice and garnish with lots of chopped fresh parsley.

Leftover Mashed Potatoes
Serves 4

Here are 3 ways to give new life to cold mashed potatoes.

Baked
2 to 3 cups cold mashed potatoes (500 mL to 750 mL)
1/2 cup milk (125 mL)
2 eggs, beaten
1/2 teaspoon salt (2 mL)
1/2 cup grated Swiss cheese (or Parmesan) (125 mL)

Combine the potatoes, milk, eggs and salt. Pour into a buttered 8 inch square (2 L) baking pan and sprinkle with the cheese. Bake in a 350°F (180°C) oven for 30 minutes.

Fried

Add a bit of summer savory and finely chopped onion to cold mashed potatoes. Form patties and fry them on both sides in a bit of butter. Serve with leftover roast chicken or turkey.

Pancakes

1/2 cup Bisquick (125 mL)
1 egg
1/4 cup milk (60 mL)
2 tablespoons chopped onion (30 mL)
1 cup mashed potatoes (250 mL)

Combine all the ingredients well. Drop by spoonfuls onto a greased skillet and fry until golden on both sides.

Turkey Casserole   Serves 4

You can make this in the morning and stow it in the refrigerator until you're ready to bake. Add an extra 15 minutes to the baking time if it goes into the oven cold.

1 1/2 cups broken uncooked spaghetti or vermicelli (375 mL)
1 1/2 cups cooked turkey (or chicken), cubed (375 mL)
10 ounce can condensed cream of chicken soup (284 mL)
1/2 cup chicken bouillon (or water) (125 mL)
1/4 cup chopped green pepper (optional) (60 mL)
1/4 cup chopped onion (60 mL)
1/4 cup chopped celery (60 mL)
1/2 teaspoon salt (2 mL)
1/8 teaspoon pepper (0.5 mL)
1 1/2 cups grated Cheddar cheese (375 mL)

Cook the spaghetti or vermicelli according to the directions on the package. Drain and rinse with cold water. Combine all the remaining ingredients with the pasta, saving 1/2 cup (125 mL) of the cheese for the top. Top with the remaining cheese. Bake, covered, in a 350°F (180°C) oven for 20 minutes. Remove the cover and bake for an additional 10 minutes.

Turkey Divan

Serves 4

10 ounce package asparagus spears (or broccoli) (275 g)
6 tablespoons grated Parmesan cheese (90 mL)
4 slices cooked turkey
  OR
8 slices cooked chicken
10 ounce can condensed cream of chicken soup (284 mL)
1/4 cup cereal cream (60 mL)
1/2 cup white wine (125 mL)
1 tablespoon butter (15 mL)

Cook the asparagus (or broccoli) according to the directions on the package. Drain well. Place the vegetable in the bottom of a greased shallow baking dish and sprinkle with 2 tablespoons (30 mL) of the Parmesan cheese. Lay the turkey (or chicken) slices on top, overlapping them.

In a saucepan combine the soup, cream and wine. Cook over low heat until smooth and well blended, stirring constantly. Pour this over the meat, covering completely. Top with the remaining Parmesan cheese and dot with butter. Bake in a 400°F (200°C) oven for 15 to 20 minutes.

The Twelfth Hole:
Breads and Muffins

Bacon, Onion and Cheese Bread   1 loaf

I have tried this bread with the ketchup and without. I prefer it with. It doesn't have a "ketchupy" flavor but it definitely complements the wonderful bacon-cheese-onion flavor.

1/2 cup softened butter (125 mL)
2 tablespoons ketchup (30 mL)
2 tablespoons finely chopped green onion (30 mL)
1 1/2 cups grated mozzarella or Monterey Jack cheese (375 mL)
1 loaf French bread
2 slices bacon, uncooked

Blend the butter, ketchup, green onions and grated cheese. Cut the bread into 1 inch (2.5 cm) slices, almost through the bottom, but not quite. Spread each slice with the butter mixture. Arrange the bacon slices on top of the bread. Wrap the loaf in foil and bake in a 350°F (180°C) oven for 30 minutes. Open the foil to expose the top of the loaf. Increase the oven temperature to 400°F (200°C) and bake an additional 5 to 10 minutes. Remove bacon before serving.

Note: You may have leftover butter-cheese-onion mixture, depending on the size of your French loaf. Use it the following week on split hamburger buns. Spead each cut surface of bun and place under the broiler until bubbly. Nice with soup or salad at lunchtime.

Hot Cheese Bread

1 loaf

I like to keep a loaf of French bread cut in half lengthwise in the freezer. It is easier to spread butter on the frozen cut surface than on a too fresh one.

1 loaf French bread, cut in half lengthwise
butter or margarine
Parmesan cheese

Spread each cut side of French bread fairly liberally with butter, then sprinkle lightly with Parmesan cheese. Wrap foil around the crust but leave the cheese-sprinkled surfaces *unwrapped*. Bake in a 350°F (180°C) oven for 20 to 25 minutes or until the tops are golden. Remove from the oven and cut into serving pieces.

Health Bread

1 loaf

This very heavy bread is like some of the Russian breads. Sliced thinly, it is a perfect "bed" for smoked salmon. Spread with cream cheese or any cheese spread, it makes a nutritious lunch or between-meal snack. It is very satisfying and sooo easy!

2 teaspoons baking soda (10 mL)
2 tablespoons molasses (30 mL)
3 cups boiling water (750 mL)
3 cups Red River cereal (750 mL)
2 teaspoons salt (10 mL)
1 cup whole wheat flour (250 mL)

In a large mixing bowl stir the soda into the molasses and add the boiling water. Stir in the cereal, salt and flour in that order. Beat at high speed for 2 minutes. Cover and let sit overnight or all day at room temperature. Pour into a greased loaf pan and smooth the top. Bake in a 275°F (135°C) oven for 1 hour. Reduce the heat to 250°F (130°C) and bake an additional 1 hour.

Cool, wrap in foil and store in the refrigerator for 1 day before slicing.

Irish Soda Bread

1 round loaf

This can be made very quickly and easily. It is nice toasted the next day.

3 cups sifted all-purpose flour (750 mL)
1 1/4 teaspoons baking soda (6 mL)
1/2 teaspoon cream of tartar (2 mL)
1/2 teaspoon salt (2 mL)
2 tablespoons melted butter (30 mL)
1 1/2 cups buttermilk (375 mL)

Sift the dry ingredients into a large bowl and make a well in the center. Add the melted butter and buttermilk and stir with a wooden spoon to make a soft dough. Turn the dough out onto a lightly floured board and knead gently—about 1 minute, just until the dough holds its shape and is no longer sticky. (This dough requires neither kneading nor rising as yeast breads do.) Shape the dough into a round loaf and place it on a lightly buttered baking sheet. Bake in a 400°F (200°C) oven for 40 minutes.

Quick Whole Wheat Bread

1 loaf

Home-baked bread in 1 hour and 5 minutes — 1 hour to bake it, 5 minutes to assemble it.

2 1/4 cups whole wheat flour (560 mL)
1 1/2 tablespoons sugar (22 mL)
1 teaspoon salt (5 mL)
2 teaspoons baking powder (10 mL)
1/4 teaspoon baking soda (1 mL)
12 ounces freshly opened club soda or beer (375 mL)
2 teaspoons sesame seeds (10 mL)

Stir all the dry ingredients together *except* the sesame seeds. Add the club soda (or beer) and combine well. Pour the batter into a buttered loaf pan, sprinkle sesame seeds on top and bake in a 350°F (180°C) oven for 1 hour.

Dumplings

7 or 8 dumplings

If you have never made dumplings for stew, I couldn't introduce you to an easier recipe than this one.

1 cup all-purpose flour (250 mL)
1 tablespoon baking powder (15 mL)
1/2 teaspoon salt (2 mL)
1 1/2 tablespoons oil (22 mL)
2/3 cup milk (150 mL)

Sift the flour, baking powder and salt into mixing bowl. Combine the oil and milk and add this to the dry ingredients. Stir only until just blended. Drop by a large spoon over simmering stew. Cover tightly. Simmer for 15 minutes. Serve at once.

Note: As a variation for beef stew try adding 1 tablespoon (15 mL) of chopped parsley to the flour mixture. For chicken stew you can add 1 tablespoon (15 mL) cooked and crumbled bacon or 1/4 teaspoon (1 mL) summer savory to the flour mixture.

Pineapple Carrot Muffins

1 dozen large muffins

If you want to make the currently popular "giant" muffins you can use greased custard cups.

2 eggs
1/2 cup vegetable oil (125 mL)
1 teaspoon vanilla (5 mL)
1 cup finely grated carrot (250 mL)
1/2 cup crushed pineapple, with juice (125 mL)
1 1/2 cups all-purpose flour (375 mL)
1/2 cup sugar (125 mL)
1 teaspoon baking powder (5 mL)
1 teaspoon baking soda (5 mL)
1 teaspoon cinnamon (5 mL)
1/2 teaspoon salt (2 mL)

Beat the eggs into the oil and vanilla. Stir in the grated carrots and pineapple. Sift all the other ingredients together and add this to the first mixture. Mix just until all the flour is absorbed. Fill muffin tins 2/3 full and bake for 20 minutes in a preheated 350°F (180°C) oven.

Pumpkin Muffins

1 dozen large muffins

I often have canned pumpkin left over when I make pumpkin pie or pumpkin soup. This is a great way of using it.

1 cup canned pumpkin (250 mL)
1/4 teaspoon baking soda (1 mL)
1/2 cup margarine (125 mL)
1 1/4 cups sugar (310 mL)
2 large eggs
2 1/4 cups flour (560 mL)
2 1/2 teaspoons baking powder (12 mL)
1/2 teaspoon cinnamon (2 mL)
1/2 teaspoon ginger (2 mL)
1/2 teaspoon nutmeg (2 mL)
dash of salt

Combine the pumpkin and baking soda. Cream the margarine with the sugar. Add the eggs, one at a time, beating after each addition. Sift the dry ingredients together and add to the margarine mixture alternately with the pumpkin. Do not overmix. Spoon the batter into greased muffin tins. Bake in a 375°F (190°C) oven for about 20 minutes.

Pizza Crust

1 crust

I was going to put this recipe in the Ultra Easy section where there are a number of quick and easy recipes, but I thought it might be overlooked by cooks who will find it very useful. If you have teenage children, they can make this themselves.

1 cup flour (250 mL)
3 tablespoons mayonnaise (45 mL)
1/2 cup milk (125 mL)

Mix all the ingredients together. Knead in a little extra flour — about 1 to 2 tablespoons (15 mL to 30 mL). Using your fingers, spread the dough in a pie plate. Fill with your favorite pizza mixture and bake.

Chocolate Zucchini Bread   2 loaves

If you have zucchini in your garden, you know how prolific it is. This is just one good way to use it — check the Index for several other excellent ideas.

3 large eggs
2 cups sugar (500 mL)
1 cup salad oil (250 mL)
2 squares bitter chocolate, melted
1 teaspoon vanilla (5 mL)
2 cups peeled, grated zucchini (500 mL)
3 cups flour (750 mL)
2 teaspoons cocoa (10 mL)
1 teaspoon salt (5 mL)
1 teaspoon cinnamon (5 mL)
1 teaspoon baking soda (5 mL)
1 1/2 teaspoons baking powder (7 mL)
2/3 cup nuts (optional) (150 mL)

Beat the eggs until light. Beat in the sugar and oil. Stir in the chocolate, vanilla and grated zucchini. Sift the flour, cocoa, salt, cinnamon, baking soda and baking powder and add this to the egg-chocolate mixture. Stir in the nuts. Pour this batter into 2 loaf pans and bake in a 350°F (180°C) oven for 1 hour, or until a toothpick inserted in the center comes out clean.

Marlene Rayner's Quick Coffee Cake
                                                                    1 cake

3/4 cup sugar (175 mL)
1 1/4 cups flour (310 mL)
2 teaspoons baking powder (10 mL)
1/2 teaspoon salt (2 mL)
1 egg
3/4 cup milk (175 mL)

Topping
5 teaspoons cinnamon (25 mL)
2 tablespoons sugar (30 mL)
2 tablespoons brown sugar (30 mL)

Sift together the sugar, flour, baking powder and salt. Beat the egg into the milk and combine well with the dry ingredients. Pour this batter into an 8 inch (1.2 L) round cake pan. Combine the topping ingredients and sprinkle this mixture on top of the batter. Bake in a 450°F (230°C) oven for 10 to 15 minutes.

Serve hot with a bit of melted butter drizzled over each cut wedge.

Bran Muffins 3 1/2 dozen muffins

This batter will keep for 3 weeks in the refrigerator. Frozen and reheated muffins are fine, but freshly baked from the oven to you can't be beat. If you are called upon to donate something to a bake sale, these are perfect. There are enough for the bake sale and you, too!

2 1/2 cups sugar (625 mL)
2/3 cup margarine (150 mL)
3 large eggs
4 cups flour (1 L)
1 tablespoon salt (15 mL)
2 1/2 tablespoons baking powder (37 mL)
3 cups 100% natural wheat bran (750 mL)
3 cups buttermilk (750 mL)
14 ounce can crushed pineapple, drained (398 mL)
1 1/2 cups raisins (375 mL)
1/2 cup boiling water (125 mL)
1 tablespoon baking soda (15 mL)

Cream the sugar and margarine. Add the eggs one at a time, beating well after each addition. Combine the flour, salt, baking powder and bran and add this to the sugar-margarine mixture alternately with the buttermilk. Stir in the crushed pineapple and raisins. Lastly combine the baking soda with the boiling water and add this to the batter. Refrigerate for 24 hours. Bake in a 400°F (200°C) oven for 20 minutes.

Note: If you want to make "giant" muffins, such as those sold in the muffin specialty shops, use greased custard cups.

The Thirteenth Hole: Cakes and Frostings

Carolyn's Cherry Cake

Serves 10 to 12

A great family friend gives this cake to my husband every Christmas and he *hides* it. Now I ask you — is this the Christmas spirit?

1 cup butter (250 mL)
1 cup sugar (250 mL)
3 eggs
2 1/4 cups sifted flour (560 mL)
1/4 teaspoon salt (1 mL)
1 large bottle maraschino cherries, drained

Cream the butter and add the sugar gradually. Add the eggs, one at a time, beating well after each addition. Flour the cherries with some of the flour and add them to the butter mixture. Add the flour and salt. Bake in a tube pan (with a large hole) in a 300°F (150°C) oven for 1 hour.

Sheila's Chocolate Cake

Serves 12

While visiting a friend in Calgary I was asked, "Do you want a terrific recipe for chocolate cake?" I politely answered, "No, thanks — I have two in my book now," whereupon she replied, "Well, I am going to give it to you anyway because it is *so* good." She was right — not only good but easy!

1 package devil's food cake mix (520 g)
1 package instant pudding (vanilla or chocolate) (92 g)
1/2 cup vegetable oil (125 mL)
1/2 cup warm water (125 mL)
4 large eggs
1 1/2 teaspoons cinnamon (7 mL)
1/2 teaspoon cloves (2 mL)
1 cup sour cream (250 mL)
6 ounce package chocolate chips (175 g)

Place all the ingredients *except* the chocolate chips in a large mixing bowl. Blend well, then beat on medium speed for 4 minutes. Fold in the chocolate chips. Pour into a greased and floured 10 inch (3 L) angel food pan. Bake in a 350°F (180°C) oven for 55 to 60 minutes.

Note: This cake is best served warm, while the chocolate chips are still gooey. You can leave it in the pan until you are ready to serve, which will lengthen the cooling time.

Coconut Hot Milk Cake   Serves 4 to 6

If you have celebrated your 39th birthday 10 times as I have, you will remember your mother's "hot milk cake" from when you were growing up. It was making the rounds at about that time.

2 eggs
1 cup flour (250 mL)
1 cup sugar (250 mL)
1 teaspoon baking powder (5 mL)
1/2 teaspoon salt (2 mL)
1/2 cup milk (125 mL)
2 tablespoons butter (30 mL)
1/2 teaspoon vanilla (2 mL)

Beat the eggs. Sift the flour, sugar, baking powder and salt together and add this mixture to the eggs. Heat the milk to boiling and add the butter. Stir until the butter has melted, then stir the milk and butter into the eggs and flour along with the vanilla. Pour into an 8 inch (2 L) square pan and bake in a 350°F (180°C) oven for 30 minutes. Let cool while you make the following icing.

Icing
3 tablespoons butter (45 mL)
5 tablespoons brown sugar (75 mL)
2 tablespoons cereal cream (30 mL)
3/4 cup coconut (175 mL)

Combine all the ingredients and bring to a boil. Boil for 2 minutes. Spread on the slightly cooled cake and brown under the broiler — about 3 minutes.

Coffee Rum Cake   Serves 12

Who has time to make a cake from scratch during the golfing season?
If you prefer a *chocolate* rum cake, see the Note. If you can't decide
which to make, make both. You now have dessert for 20 people!

1 cup chopped pecans (250 mL)
1 package white or golden cake mix (520 g)
1 package instant vanilla pudding (92 g)
4 large eggs
1/2 cup cold water (125 mL)
1/2 cup oil (125 mL)
1/2 cup rum (or brandy) (125 mL)

Grease and flour a 10 inch (3 L) tube or bundt pan. Sprinkle the pecans
over the bottom of the pan. In a large mixing bowl, combine the remaining ingredients and beat for 5 minutes on medium speed. Pour the
batter over the nuts and bake in a preheated 350°F (180°C) oven for
50 to 60 minutes.

Cool the cake in the pan. Invert, poke holes in the cake with a toothpick or skewer and brush the top and sides with the following glaze.
Brush on more glaze as the first application soaks in.

Glaze
1/4 cup butter (60 mL)
1 cup sugar (250 mL)
1/4 cup strong black coffee (60 mL) (about 1 tablespoon—15 mL instant)
1/2 cup rum (125 mL)

Melt the butter. Stir in the sugar and coffee. Boil for 5 minutes, stirring
occasionally. Remove from the heat and stir in the rum. (If I am making
this for my family, I cut the glaze in half. It is not so baba-like—soaked.)

Decorate the top of the cake with whipped cream and toasted slivered almonds just before serving.

Note: For a Chocolate Rum Cake, substitute chocolate cake mix for
the white or golden and use walnuts instead of pecans.

Chocolate Zucchini Cake

Serves 12

3/4 cup butter (or margarine) (175 mL)
2 cups sugar (500 mL)
3 eggs
2 1/2 cups flour (625 mL)
1/2 cup cocoa (125 mL)
1 1/2 teaspoons baking soda (7 mL)
2 1/2 teaspoons baking powder (12 mL)
1 teaspoon salt (5 mL)
1 teaspoon cinnamon (5 mL)
3 cups unpeeled, grated zucchini (750 mL)
2 teaspoons grated orange rind (10 mL)
2 teaspoons vanilla (10 mL)
1/2 cup chopped nuts (125 mL)

Cream the butter and sugar. Add the eggs one at a time, beating well after each addition. Sift the dry ingredients together and add to the butter, sugar and eggs. The batter will be stiff at this stage. Stir in the zucchini, orange rind and vanilla and nuts. Pour into a well-greased and floured tube pan* and bake for 1 hour in a 350°F (180°C) oven.

Note: If you want to dress this cake up a little, "frost" with the following glaze.

* If you have no tube pan, use a 9 by 13 inch (3.5 L) oblong baking pan and reduce the baking time by 15 minutes.

Glaze
2 cups icing sugar (500 mL)
1 teaspoon grated orange rind (5 mL)
1/4 cup orange juice (60 mL)

Stir all together until smooth and pour over the cooled cake.

Gingerbread

Serves 12

How do you beat warm gingerbread and whipped cream?

1 cup molasses (250 mL)
2 cups applesauce (500 mL)
2 teaspoons baking soda (10 mL)
4 large eggs
1 1/3 cups sugar (325 mL)
2/3 cup oil (150 mL)
3 cups sifted flour (750 mL)
1 teaspoon salt (5 mL)
2 teaspoons ginger (10 mL)
2 teaspoons cinnamon (10 mL)
1/4 teaspoon cloves (1 mL)

In a saucepan stir the molasses into the applesauce and bring to a boil. Remove from the heat and stir in the soda. Set aside to cool.

Beat the eggs in a large mixing bowl until light in color. Gradually beat in the sugar and continue beating until thick. Gradually beat in the oil. Sift the dry ingredients together and fold in alternately with the cooled applesauce mixture.

Pour the batter into a greased and floured 10 inch (3 L) angel food pan and bake in a 325°F (160°C) oven for 1 hour and 20 minutes — or until a toothpick inserted in the center comes out clean. Cool in the pan for 15 minutes then remove to a rack.

Serve with whipped cream.

Note: This cake stays fresh for 6 to 7 days, but it makes a large cake. You may want to cut it in half when cool and freeze half.

Cousin Jean's Pound Cake

Serves 8

Pound cake has always been a favorite of ours. This is without a doubt the easiest and best I have ever tried. When we hadn't had this cake for some time, my teenage son said, "Mom, if you don't have time to make a pound cake, just show me how and I'll make one." Now this was from a boy whose only venture in the kitchen to date had been to open a box of cornflakes!

1 cup butter or margarine (250 mL)
1 1/2 cups white sugar (375 mL)
break in a large egg
1/2 cup warm milk (125 mL)
break in a large egg
1 cup presifted flour (250 mL)
break in a large egg
Mix and add:
1 cup presifted flour (250 mL)
1 teaspoon baking powder (5 mL)
1/2 teaspoon salt (2 mL)
break in a large egg
1 teaspoon vanilla (5 mL)
   OR
1/2 teaspoon almond extract (2 mL)

Cream the butter and sugar, then add all the remaining ingredients *in the order given*, beating *well* after each addition. No need to sift the flour if you use the presifted. Pour the batter into a 9 by 5 inch (2 L) loaf pan lined with waxed paper. Bake in a preheated 350°F (180°C) oven for 60 to 70 minutes.

Chocolate Frosting   For an 8 inch (2 L) square cake

How can something so easy be so good?

6 ounce package *milk* chocolate chips (175 g)
1/2 cup sour cream (125 mL)
pinch of salt

Melt the chocolate chips in the top of a double boiler. Remove from the heat and stir in the sour cream and salt. Stir until smooth.

Note: For spice cake use butterscotch chips.

Coconut Nut Frosting   For a double layer cake

Two easy ways to dress carrot cake, spice cake or apple cake.

Cooked
1/4 cup margarine (60 mL)
2 tablespoons flour (30 mL)
1 cup sugar (250 mL)
1 cup chopped nuts (250 mL)
1 cup coconut
1 cup evaporated milk (250 mL)

Melt the margarine and stir in the flour until blended. Add all the remaining ingredients and boil for 10 minutes. Let cool slightly, then pour over warm cake.

Uncooked
1/2 cup butter or margarine (125 mL)
8 ounce package cream cheese (250 g)
1 pound package icing sugar (450 g)
1 teaspoon vanilla (5 mL)
1 cup chopped nuts (250 mL)
1/2 cup coconut (125 mL)

Combine the butter and cheese and beat until light. Gradually add the sugar. Add the vanilla, nuts and coconut and mix well.

Mocha Icing

For an 8 inch (2 L) square cake

4 tablespoons butter (60 mL)
1/4 teaspoon salt (1 mL)
2 tablespoons cocoa (30 mL)
2 cups icing sugar (500 mL)
3 to 4 tablespoons hot coffee (45 mL to 60 mL)

Cream the butter, salt and cocoa. Beat in 1/2 cup (125 mL) of the icing sugar and cream well together. Alternately add the hot coffee and the remaining sugar. Beat well.

Chopped nuts sprinkled on the iced cake are a nice touch.

Whipped Cream Icing

For an 8 inch (2 L) square cake

1 cup whipping cream (250 mL)
1/4 cup icing sugar (60 mL)
1 egg white, beaten stiff
few grains of salt
1/2 teaspoon vanilla (2 mL)

Beat the cream until stiff. Slowly fold in the sugar. Fold in the egg white, salt and vanilla.

The Fourteenth Hole: Cookies

Ann Margaret's Cornflake Crisps

6 dozen crisps

When my youngest daughter was 10, I would let her make cookies — a great "boredom reliever." We went through a few disasters (caught a few spatulas in the beaters, spilled sugar on the floor which we stepped in for two days even though our budding Ann Pillsbury swore she swept it all up), but now at age 13, she is the best darned cookie maker around. The following is one of her more recent efforts.

1 cup butter or margarine (250 mL)
1 cup white sugar (250 mL)
1 cup brown sugar (250 mL)
2 eggs
1 teaspoon vanilla (5 mL)
2 cups flour (500 mL)
1 teaspoon baking soda (5 mL)
1/2 teaspoon baking powder (2 mL)
1/2 teaspoon salt (2 mL)
1/2 cup coconut (125 mL)
4 cups cornflakes (1 L)

Cream the butter and sugars. Add the eggs and beat well. Add the vanilla. Sift the flour, baking soda, baking powder and salt. Add this to the creamed mixture. Add the coconut. Stir in the cornflakes. Drop by spoonfuls, 2 inches (5 cm) apart, onto an ungreased cookie sheet. Bake in a 350°F (180°C) oven for 10 to 12 minutes, or until lightly browned.

Crisp Ginger Snaps

9 dozen snaps

1 cup butter (250 mL)
1/3 cup sugar (75 mL)
3 cups flour (750 mL)
2 teaspoons ginger (10 mL)
2 teaspoons baking soda (10 mL)
pinch of salt
2/3 cup molasses (150 mL)

Cream the butter and sugar. Sift together the dry ingredients and add them to the butter-sugar mixture alternately with the molasses. Form the dough into rolls and chill. Slice the chilled loaves thinly and bake the snaps in a 400°F (200°C) oven for 10 to 12 minutes.

Orange Slices

4 1/2 dozen slices

My mother, who used to turn out cookies as regularly as a commercial baker, swears that any cookie recipe containing both cream of tartar *and* baking soda is a surefire winner.

1/2 cup white sugar (125 mL)
1/2 cup brown sugar (125 mL)
1/2 cup butter (125 mL)
1/2 cup shortening (125 mL)
1 egg, slightly beaten
grated rind of 1 orange
2 cups flour (500 mL)
1 teaspoon cream of tartar (5 mL)
1/2 teaspoon baking soda (2 mL)
1/2 teaspoon salt (2 mL)
1 teaspoon vanilla (5 mL)

Mix all the ingredients together in the order given. Shape the dough into small balls and press each down with a fork dipped in milk. Bake in a 350°F (180°C) oven for about 12 minutes.

Graham Cracker Almond Cookies 52 bars

"Do you want the recipe for a super-easy, super-tasting cookie?" I was asked at the top of my backswing during a golf game last summer. "You bet," I answered as my ball popped up in the air and landed 10 feet in front of us!

1 cup *butter* (250 mL)
3/4 cup brown sugar (175 mL)
graham crackers
3 1/2 ounces sliced almonds (100 g)

Melt the butter and combine it with the brown sugar. Boil gently for 5 minutes. Line a jelly roll pan (cookie sheet with sides) with well-buttered foil. Line the pan with whole graham crackers. Spread the almonds on top of the crackers. Pour the butter mixture over the crackers and almonds. Bake in a 350°F (180°C) oven for 10 minutes. Remove from the oven and immediately cut each cracker in half. Cool before removing the bars from the pan.

Mother's Shortbread — The Very Best
4 dozen

The first time I made these, I told my mother they were tough. She asked, "Did you do exactly as I said?" I answered, "No, I used the mixmaster instead of mixing by hand." She shook her head and said, "You are 35 years of age and you *still* can't do as you are told."

4 cups flour (1 L)
1 cup *berry* sugar (250 mL)
1 pound butter, softened (450 g)

Mix all the ingredients *by hand* (get right in and squish with your fingers!), adding the flour and sugar to the butter gradually. Sprinkle a bit of flour on a board and pat the dough into a square, about 1/4 inch (7 mm) thick, and cut into diagonal pieces. Prick lightly with a fork. Bake in a 300°F (150°C) oven for 20 minutes.

Snow Balls

About 50 balls

Fudgy and addicting. Nice gift at Christmastime. And don't overlook the white chocolate Christmas cookie in Ultra Easy — Desserts.

6 ounce package chocolate chips (175 g)
6 ounce package butterscotch chips (175 g)
8 ounce package cream cheese (250 g)
2 cups miniature marshmallows (500 mL)
1 cup chopped walnuts (250 mL)
desiccated coconut

Melt the first 4 ingredients in a double boiler and stir in the walnuts. Chill. Form small balls and roll each in desiccated coconut. Stored in the refrigerator, these will last 4 to 6 weeks.

The Fifteenth Hole: Squares

Butter Tart Squares

16 squares

Base
1/2 cup margarine (125 mL)
1 cup flour (250 mL)
2 tablespoons brown sugar (30 mL)

Cut the margarine into the flour and brown sugar until crumbly. Press this mixture into a buttered 9 inch (2.5 L) square pan and bake in a 350°F (180°C) oven for 15 minutes.

Filling
2 eggs, beaten
1 1/2 cups brown sugar (375 mL)
1/2 cup oatmeal (125 mL)
1/2 teaspoon baking powder (2 mL)
1/4 teaspoon salt (1 mL)
1 teaspoon vanilla (5 mL)
1/2 cup chopped walnuts (125 mL)

Combine all the ingredients well and pour this mixture over the baked base. Return to the oven and bake for 20 to 25 minutes. Cool before cutting into squares.

Coconut Bars

36 bars

Easy and good for a large group!

Base
1 1/4 cups graham wafer crumbs (310 mL)
1/2 cup butter (125 mL)
1 tablespoon flour (15 mL)
1/2 cup brown sugar (125 mL)

Combine the crumbs and butter — use a mixer or rub butter into the crumbs with your fingers. Mix in the sugar and flour. Wet your fingers so the crumbs won't stick and pat the mixture into a buttered 9 by 13 inch (3.5 L) oblong pan. Bake in a 350°F (180°C) oven for 15 minutes.

Filling
1 can sweetened condensed milk (300 mL)
2 cups flaked coconut (500 mL)
1 teaspoon vanilla (5 mL)

Combine all the ingredients and spread this mixture over the Base layer. Return to the oven for 20 minutes.

Frosting
1 1/2 cups brown sugar (375 mL)
6 tablespoons cereal cream (90 mL)
1/4 cup butter (60 mL)
3/4 cup chocolate chips (175 mL)

Combine the brown sugar, cream and butter. Bring to a rolling boil and boil for 1 minute. Remove from the heat and stir in the chocolate chips. Stir until melted then spread over the coconut mixture while hot.
    Cool and cut into bars.

Date Squares

16 squares

A *little* time-consuming, but they are the best I have tried, so I had to tell you about them.

Shortbread Base
1 1/2 cups flour (375 mL)
1 teaspoon baking powder (5 mL)
1/2 teaspoon baking soda (2 mL)
1/4 teaspoon salt (1 mL)
1 cup butter (250 mL)
1 cup brown sugar (250 mL)
1 1/2 cups rolled oats (*not instant*) (375 mL)

Sift the flour, baking powder, baking soda and salt. Rub the butter into the flour mixture with your fingertips. Add the sugar and oats and mix well.

Spread half the crumbs in the bottom of a greased, shallow 9 inch (2.5 L) square pan. Pat to smooth. Cover with the date filling, then cover with the remaining crumbs. Pat to smooth. Bake in a 325°F (160°C) oven for 30 to 35 minutes, then increase the heat slightly for a few minutes to brown the top lightly.

Cut in squares while hot. Let cool in the pan.

Date Filling
1 pound chopped dates (450 g)
1 cup cold water (250 mL)
4 tablespoons brown sugar (60 mL)
grated rind of 1 orange
4 tablespoons orange juice (60 mL)
2 teaspoons lemon juice (10 mL)

Cook the dates, water, brown sugar and orange rind in a small saucepan over medium heat until thick and smooth. Remove from the heat and add the fruit juices. Mix well and cool before spreading over the shortbread base.

Terry's Lemon Squares

16 squares

These were just plain lemon squares until friend Terry was invited for dinner one evening. I had made two pans of these squares — one for dinner and one for the freezer. I won't tell you how many squares this chap ate, but there were no squares for the freezer. We have always referred to them as Terry's Lemon Squares since that time.

Shortbread Base
1 cup flour (250 mL)
1/2 cup butter or margarine (125 mL)
1/4 cup icing sugar (60 mL)

Mix all the ingredients until crumbly (a mixmaster or food processor is the easiest way). Press this mixture into the bottom of an 8 inch (2 L) square pan and bake in a 350°F (180°C) oven for 20 minutes. Let cool while you make the Lemon Topping.

Lemon Topping
1 cup sugar (250 mL)
2 tablespoons flour (30 mL)
2 eggs, slightly beaten
2 tablespoons lemon juice (30 mL)
2 teaspoons grated lemon peel (10 mL)

Mix the sugar and flour. Combine the eggs, lemon juice and lemon rind and add this to the sugar-flour mixture. Pour this over the cooked crust and bake an additional 25 minutes. Cool in pan then cut into squares.

Walnut Dreams

16 squares

Base
1/2 cup butter (125 mL)
1 cup flour (250 mL)
3 tablespoons icing sugar (45 mL)

Mix all 3 ingredients and spread the mixture in the bottom of an 8 inch (2 L) square pan. Bake in a 350°F (180°C) oven for 10 to 15 minutes.

Filling
2 eggs
1 1/2 cups brown sugar (375 mL)
1 tablespoon flour (15 mL)
1/2 teaspoon baking powder (2 mL)
1/2 cup walnuts (125 mL)
1/2 cup coconut (125 mL)

Beat the eggs and brown sugar together. Mix the flour and baking powder and add this to the eggs and sugar. Fold in the nuts and coconut. Spread this mixture over the base and bake in a 325°F (160°C) oven for 20 to 25 minutes. Let cool, then frost with Lemon Frosting.

Lemon Frosting
2 tablespoons soft butter (30 mL)
2 1/2 cups sifted icing sugar (625 mL)
2 tablespoons orange juice (30 mL)
1 tablespoon lemon juice (15 mL)

Cream the butter, gradually add the sugar alternately with the combined fruit juices. Beat to a spreading consistency.

The Sixteenth Hole: Pies

Easy Pastry

2 double crusts

This is a pastry I recommend to those who are new to the art of pastry making or who have made several unsuccessful attempts. If you are making several pies, this recipe doubles well. Any remaining portion can be stored in a plastic bag in the refrigerator and used later. (Let it come to room temperature before rolling it out.)

1/2 pound lard (225 g)
1/2 cup boiling water (125 mL)
3 cups flour (750 mL)
1 teaspoon baking powder (5 mL)
1 teaspoon salt (5 mL)

Let the lard reach room temperature, then place it in a large bowl and break it up with a fork. Add the boiling water and beat with a mixer until fluffy. Combine the flour, baking powder and salt. Add the dry ingredients to the lard mixture. Form the dough into a ball. Let it cool before rolling it out.

Note: I use Mapleleaf Tenderflake lard for all my pastry—sounds like a commercial, but it isn't. I just don't get the same results with any of the other brands I have tried.

Mother's Pastry

2 double crusts

3 cups flour (750 mL)
1 teaspoon salt (5 mL)
10 1/2 ounces lard (2/3 of a package) (300 g)
1 egg
1 teaspoon fresh lemon juice or vinegar (5 mL)

Sift the flour with the salt. Cut in the lard with a pastry blender. Place
the egg in a measuring cup and add enough water to make 1/2 cup
(125 mL). Add the lemon juice (or vinegar) to the egg and water. Stir
the liquids into the flour-lard mixture. Form the dough into a ball and
let it sit in the refrigerator for 30 minutes — no longer than an hour.

Peach Pecan Pie

Serves 6

I have tried pies designed to reduce the calorie intake, but they are
never as popular as the "loaded" ones. When I serve the following,
there is never a crumb left.

14 ounce can peach halves (398 mL)
9 inch unbaked pie shell (1 L)
1/4 cup melted butter (60 mL)
1/2 cup brown sugar (125 mL)
2 tablespoons flour (30 mL)
1/2 cup corn syrup (125 mL)
1 egg, slightly beaten
1 tablespoon lemon juice (15 mL)
1 cup pecan halves (250 mL)

Drain the peach halves very well and arrange them on the bottom of
the pie shell. Combine all the remaining ingredients *except* the pecan
halves and pour this mixture over the peaches. Arrange the pecan halves
on top. Bake in a 400°F (200°C) oven for 10 minutes. Reduce the
heat to 375°F (190°C) and continue baking for an additional 30 minutes. Serve slightly warm.

George's Coconut Cream Pie   Serves 6

So named because it is my husband's favorite (not that he makes it). Because it is so simple, he gets it fairly regularly—particularly if I have a prebaked pie shell in the freezer.

2 cups milk (500 mL)
4 tablespoons cornstarch (scant) (60 mL)
1/2 cup coconut (125 mL)
1/3 cup sugar (75 mL)
1/2 teaspoon salt (2 mL)
3 large egg yolks
1 tablespoon butter (15 mL)
1 teaspoon vanilla (5 mL)

9 inch baked pie shell (1 L)

Mix 2 tablespoons (30 mL) of the milk with the cornstarch and set aside. Scald the remaining milk, then mix it with the coconut in the top of a double boiler. When the mixture is hot, stir in the sugar, salt and cornstarch. Add a little of the hot mixture to the yolks, then stir them in. Cook, stirring constantly, until the mixture is thick. Stir in the butter and vanilla. Cool slightly then pour into a baked pie shell. Top with meringue and bake as directed below.

Meringue
3 egg whites
3 tablespoons sugar (45 mL)
1/2 teaspoon baking powder (2 mL)
1 tablespoon coconut (15 mL)

Beat the egg whites until they form soft peaks. Mix the sugar and baking powder and gradually add this to the egg whites. Spread the meringue on a filled pie shell and sprinkle the top with coconut. Bake in a 300°F (150°C) oven for about 15 minutes, or until nicely browned.

Lemon Pie

Serves 6

Lemon pie was the pie I had the most trouble with when I was first married. It was either too runny or too stiff and I couldn't get a packaged pie filling by my husband without detection. He likes it *almost* runny but still holding its shape. When I first made the following recipe he exclaimed, "Well you finally got it right!"

4 tablespoons cornstarch (60 mL)
4 tablespoons flour (60 mL)
1/2 teaspoon salt (2 mL)
1 1/2 cups sugar (375 mL)
1 1/2 cups boiling water (375 mL)
4 egg yolks, slightly beaten
1 tablespoon butter (15 mL)
few gratings of lemon rind
1/3 cup lemon juice (75 mL)
9 inch baked pie shell (1 L)
3 egg whites
1/4 teaspoon cream of tartar (1 mL)
1/3 cup granulated sugar (75 mL)

In a saucepan combine the cornstarch, flour, salt and sugar. Gradually add the boiling water. Cook over medium heat, stirring constantly, until thickened. Stir a small amount of the hot mixture into the slightly beaten egg yolks, then blend them into the remaining hot mixture. Cook 1 or 2 minutes longer, stirring constantly. Remove from the heat and blend in the butter, lemon rind and lemon juice. Cool to lukewarm and turn into prepared pie shell.

Top with meringue: beat the egg whites until frothy, add the cream of tartar, then gradually add the sugar and continue beating until stiff. Pile lightly on top of the pie, completely covering the filling. Bake in a 400°F (200°C) oven for 5 minutes or until meringue is golden. Cool at room temperature.

Joyce's Meringue Pie

Serves 6

I told Joyce I wouldn't be quite as dejected every time her ball passes mine "on the fly" (which is every time we play) if she would give me the recipe for her meringue pie!

4 egg whites
pinch of cream of tartar
pinch of salt
1/4 teaspoon vanilla (1 mL)
3/4 cup sugar (175 mL)

Beat the egg whites until frothy. Add the cream of tartar and beat again. Add the salt and vanilla. Beat on medium-high while adding the sugar 1/2 teaspoon (2 mL) at a time until peaks form—about 5 minutes. Oil a 10 inch (1.5 L) glass pie plate. Mound the meringue and sweep it to the outer edges to a thickness of 1 1/2 inches (4 cm) above the rim. Bake in a 200°F (100°C) oven for 2 hours on the middle shelf. Cool.

Filling
4 egg yolks
1/2 cup sugar (125 mL)
1 tablespoon lemon juice (15 mL)
3 tablespoons Grand Marnier (45 mL)
1 cup heavy cream, whipped (250 mL)
toasted almonds (garnish)

Combine the egg yolks and sugar in a double boiler. Blend with a wire whisk for about 10 minutes over moderate heat until the yolks thicken to a smooth, mayonnaise-like consistency. Do not cook them too quickly or they will curdle. Remove from the heat and stir in the lemon juice and Grand Marnier. When quite cool, fold in the whipped cream. Refrigerate for at least 3 hours. Spoon the mixture into the cooled meringue and garnish with slivered almonds.

Homemade Mincemeat Pie
For 5 9-inch (1 L) pies

This is a wonderful way to use up the green tomato "harvest" — the ones you pick when Jack Frost is about to bite. If I didn't have any green tomatoes, I would buy them just to make this recipe. (Supermarkets usually have green tomatoes in the back where they are kept to ripen.) I have tried many recipes for mincemeat over the years and this is by far the best.

Mincemeat
3 quarts green tomatoes, chopped (3 L)
1 quart apples, chopped (1 L)
1/2 pound butter (225 g)
2 1/2 pounds dark brown sugar (1.25 kg)
1 pound raisins (450 g)
1 cup vinegar (250 mL)
1/2 pound mixed peel (used for fruitcakes) (225 g)
1 tablespoon salt (15 mL)
1 tablespoon cinnamon (15 mL)
1 tablespoon cloves (15 mL)
1 tablespoon nutmeg (15 mL)

Cover the chopped tomatoes with water and boil for 15 minutes. Strain and leave all night. In the morning, add the apples, butter, sugar, raisins, vinegar, mixed peel and salt. Simmer for 2 hours. Remove from the heat and add the cinnamon, cloves and nutmeg. Keep 4 cups (1 L) out for 1 pie and store the remaining mincemeat in sealers, or refrigerated for up to 6 months.

Pie
Line a pie pan with your favorite pie crust. Fill with roughly 4 cups (1 L) of the above mincemeat. (I sometimes add 1 tablespoon (15 mL) of brandy at this point.) Cover with a top crust. Bake in a 425°F (220°C) oven for 10 minutes. Reduce the temperature to 350°F (180°C) and bake an additional 20 to 30 minutes or until the crust has browned nicely.

Barb Chapman's Mud Pie

Serves 10

I had never heard of Mud Pie until 2 years ago when a girl approached me at a party and said, "I don't have your cookbook yet but Jane gave me your recipes for Cheesecake and Mud Pie and they were both super." I started sleuthing and discovered Jane thought she had gotten the Mud Pie from me but in fact she got it from Marion who got it from Barb.

Barb lives in southern California, which reinforces what I said earlier — good recipes travel very quickly!

Crust
18 Oreo chocolate cream sandwich cookies
1/3 cup melted butter (75 mL)

Crush the cookies to make fine crumbs. Stir in the melted butter. Press this mixture into the bottom and around the sides of a 9-inch (1.5 L) deep dish pie plate and chill.

Filling
1 quart coffee ice cream, slightly softened (1 L)
2 squares *unsweetened* chocolate
1 tablespoon butter (15 mL)
1/2 cup sugar (125 mL)
6 ounce (small) can evaporated milk (160 mL)

Spread the slightly softened ice cream over the crust and put it in freezer while you make the second stage of the filling.

In the top of a double boiler combine the chocolate, butter and sugar and cook slowly until melted. Slowly add the evaporated milk and cook until thickened. Chill this mixture, then spread it over the ice cream.

(If you are pressed for time, use commercial fudge sauce for the filling.)

Topping
1 tablespoon icing sugar (15 mL)
2 teaspoons Kahlua liqueur (10 mL)
　OR
1 teaspoon vanilla (5 mL)
1 cup heavy cream, whipped (250 mL)

Add the sugar and liqueur to the whipped cream and spread this topping over the pie. Freeze until serving time.

Peanut Butter Pie

Serves 6 to 8

Shortly after "chunky-style" peanut butter appeared on the scene, peanut butter pies and peanut butter cheesecakes started appearing on
menus all over the country. People had rediscovered peanut butter.
Here is a very easy pie. Fortunately the "skinny look" is out, so we can
eat things like this without feeling guilty (well not too guilty)!

3 large eggs, slightly beaten
3 tablespoons melted butter (45 mL)
1 cup sugar (250 mL)
1 cup light corn syrup (250 mL)
1 teaspoon vanilla (5 mL)
1/2 teaspoon salt (2 mL)
1/3 cup chunky-style peanut butter (75 mL)

9 inch unbaked pie shell (1 L)
whipped cream topping

Beat all the ingredients together until well blended, then fill the pie
shell. Bake in a preheated 350°F (180°C) oven for 40 to 50 minutes
or until the center is set. Chill and serve topped with whipped cream.

Note: Another method I tried was spreading a thin layer of chunky
peanut butter, 1 cup (250 mL) peanut butter mixed with 1/2 cup
(125 mL) icing sugar, over the bottom of a baked and cooled pie crust
before I filled it with banana cream pie filling and topped it with
meringue.

Schnitz Pie (Apple Pie)

Serves 6

I have two friends who constantly fight over the origin of this pie — one
says it comes from her mother, the other swears it comes from *his* mother.
They're both wrong: it comes from Mr. Justice G. Forsyth's mother and
are you going to argue with a judge?

1/2 cup flour (125 mL)
3/4 cup brown sugar (175 mL)
9 inch unbaked pie shell (1 L)
6 to 8 tart apples, peeled and cut into wedges
cinnamon
butter (to dot)
1/2 cup sour cream (125 mL)

Topping
1/3 cup flour (75 mL)
1/2 cup white sugar (125 mL)
3 tablespoons butter (45 mL)

Combine the flour and brown sugar. Sprinkle 2 tablespoons (30 mL) of this mixture over the bottom of the pie shell. Combine the remaining flour-sugar mixture with the apples and place them in the pie shell. Sprinkle lightly with cinnamon. Dot with butter and spread the sour cream in a thin layer over all.

Mix the topping ingredients until crumbly and sprinkle this mixture over the sour cream. Bake in a 450°F (230°C) oven for 10 minutes. Reduce the heat to 350°F (180°C) and bake an additional 20 to 30 minutes or until the apples are soft. Serve warm or cold.

Sheila's Pumpkin Ice Cream Pie
Serves 8 to 10

This is a very easy dessert for holiday entertaining — a nice change from the traditional pumpkin pie.

Crust
1 1/4 cups ginger snap crumbs (310 mL)
1/4 cup melted butter (60 mL)

Combine the crumbs and butter and press this mixture into the bottom and around the sides of a 10 inch (2 L) deep dish pie plate (or 9 inch — 2.5 L square baking dish). Reserve some crumbs to decorate the top of the pie.

Filling
1 quart vanilla ice cream, softened (1 L)
1 cup canned pumpkin (250 mL)
1/3 cup brown sugar (75 mL)
1/4 teaspoon salt (1 mL)
1/2 teaspoon cinnamon (2 mL)
1/2 teaspoon ginger (2 mL)
1/2 teaspoon cloves (2 mL)

Mix all the ingredients together and spread the mixture in the pie shell. Work fairly quickly as the ice cream should not get runny. Sprinkle the remaining crumbs on top and freeze all day, overnight or a week before your party. Remove the pie from the freezer 1/2 hour before serving.

Sour Cream Raisin Pie

Serves 6

They say the way to a man's heart is through his stomach. If you can't get him with this pie, he's a lost cause. (I did it with chocolate fudge — but it was my mother's.)

2 eggs, separated
1 cup brown sugar (250 mL)
2 tablespoons cornstarch (30 mL)
1 cup sour cream (250 mL)
dash of salt
1/2 teaspoon vanilla (2 mL)
1 cup raisins (250 mL)
1 tablespoon butter (15 mL)

9 inch baked pie shell (1 L)

Beat the egg yolks lightly. Mix the sugar and cornstarch and add alternately with the sour cream to the egg yolks. Add the salt, vanilla and raisins and cook the mixture in a double boiler for 25 minutes, stirring fairly regularly. Remove from the heat and stir in the butter until it is melted and absorbed. Cool. Put in a baked pie shell and top with meringue.

Meringue
2 egg whites
1/4 teaspoon cream of tartar (1 mL)
3 tablespoons sugar (45 mL)

Whip the egg whites until they are frothy then add the cream of tartar. Beat until the whites are stiff but not dry. Beat in the sugar, 1 teaspoon (5 mL) at a time. Cover the pie with meringue and bake in a 350°F (180°C) oven until lightly browned — 7 to 10 minutes.

The Seventeenth Hole: Desserts

Baked Apple Slices

Serves 6

If you are looking for a dessert to follow a hearty meal, such as pot roast or short ribs, this simple apple dessert is "just right."

6 apples
2 tablespoons butter (30 mL)
1/2 teaspoon cinnamon (2 mL)
1/2 cup sugar (125 mL)

Sauce
1/3 cup sugar (75 mL)
1 tablespoon cornstarch (15 mL)
3/4 cup water (175 mL)
1 teaspoon butter (5 mL)
1 teaspoon vanilla (5 mL)

Peel the apples, then core and quarter them. If the apples are quite large, cut them in eighths. Arrange the apples in a shallow baking dish. Dot with butter and sprinkle with cinnamon and sugar. Bake in a 350°F (180°C) oven, uncovered, for 30 minutes or until almost soft. While the apples are baking, make the sauce.

Combine the sugar, cornstarch and water. Cook over medium heat until thickened and clear. Remove the mixture from the heat and stir in the butter and vanilla. Pour this sauce over the apples and bake an additional 10 to 15 minutes or until the sauce bubbles and the apples are completely cooked. Serve warm.

Baked Bananas with Grand Marnier Sauce

Serves 4

Very popular with men!

4 medium bananas
1/2 cup honey (125 mL)
2 tablespoons butter (30 mL)
2 tablespoons Grand Marnier (30 mL)
1/4 teaspoon nutmeg (1 mL)

Cut the bananas in half lengthwise then in thirds crosswise. Arrange them in a single layer in a shallow glass baking dish (a pie plate will do). Combine the remaining ingredients. Heat the mixture until the butter has melted and pour over the bananas. Bake in a 350°F (180°C) oven for 20 minutes, or until the bananas are tender. Serve hot over ice cream.

Note: It helps to have the ice cream scooped ahead of time and sitting covered in a pretty serving dish in the freezer until needed.

Almond Cake Sorensen

Serves 8

Now that you can buy almonds already ground, this fabulous dessert is a snap.

Cake
4 egg yolks
1 cup sugar (250 mL)
2 tablespoons flour (30 mL)
1/2 teaspoon baking powder (2 mL)
1 tablespoon orange juice (15 mL)
1/2 teaspoon almond extract (2 mL)
4 egg whites
2 cups ground almonds (500 mL)

Beat the egg yolks until light. Beat in the sugar. Combine the flour and baking powder and add them to the egg yolk-sugar mixture. Mix in the orange juice and almond extract. Beat the egg whites until stiff and fold them into the above mixture. Fold in the ground almonds. Pour the whole into 2 9-inch (1.5 L) lined, round cake pans. Bake in a 350°F (180°C) oven for 25 minutes then let cool.

Filling
1/2 cup whipping cream (125 mL)
1 1/2 teaspoons grated orange rind (7 mL)

Whip the cream and stir in the orange rind. Spread this mixture between the cooled cake layers.

Topping
6 ounces semisweet chocolate chips (175 g)
1/2 cup sour cream (125 mL)

Melt the chocolate and stir in the sour cream. Spread this mixture over the top of the layer cake. Refrigerate until serving time.

Note: For a splendid Strawberry Almond Cake, pour the above cake batter into a 10 inch (3 L) lined, springform pan (*not* the tube type). Bake in a 350°F (180°C) oven for 30 to 35 minutes, or until the cake springs back when touched lightly on the top. Cool then cover the top with whole strawberries — points up. Make a glaze by combining 1 pint (500 mL) of frozen strawberries put through a strainer with 2 tablespoons (30 mL) of sugar and 1 tablespoon (15 mL) of cornstarch in a small saucepan and slowly heating the mixture until thickened. Cool the glaze and carefully spread it over the top of the berries. For a *spectacular dessert*, pipe whipped cream up and down the sides of the cake!

Banana Split Dessert

Serves 12

Not all golfers are my age (over 40 is all I will admit to). For those who are 20 years younger, run 5 miles a day after 18 holes and love desserts—do I have a dessert for you! Make the Base and the Middle in the morning then add the Top up to 2 hours before you're ready to splurge.

Base
1 1/2 cups flour (375 mL)
1/4 cup brown sugar (60 mL)
1/4 cup butter (60 mL)
1/4 cup chopped walnuts (60 mL)

Combine all the above ingredients until they are mixed to a crumbly state — like cornmeal. Press this mixture into a 9 by 13 inch (3.5 L) oblong baking pan and bake in a preheated 375°F (190°C) oven for 12 to 15 minutes. Cool.

Middle
1 cup butter (250 mL)
2 cups icing sugar (500 mL)
2 tablespoons lemon juice (30 mL)
2 eggs, beaten

Cream the butter and gradually add the icing sugar. Beat in the lemon juice and eggs. Spread this mixture over the cooled base.

Top
3 to 4 bananas
14 ounce can crushed pineapple, drained (398 mL)
1 pint fresh sliced (or well-drained frozen) strawberries (500 mL)
10 ounce can chocolate syrup (284 mL)
1 cup whipping cream, whipped (or more!) (250 mL)
1/4 to 1/2 cup chopped walnuts (60 mL to 125 mL)

Slice the bananas lengthwise and place them over the middle layer. Top with pineapple, then strawberries. Drizzle chocolate syrup over this layer then top with whipped cream. Sprinkle nuts over the top. Serve within 2 hours.

Bride's Dessert

Serves 4 to 6

So called because it was given to me as a bride by another bride and I was very grateful. It *always* turns out and with a package of Jell-O in your cupboard and ice cream in the freezer, you can have a very presentable dessert in jig time. Vary the jelly powders to suit the occasion — raspberry for Valentine's Day, lime for St. Patrick's Day, lemon for Easter. I had long forgotten about this dessert until a friend wrote to thank me for my first book and said she had blessed me frequently over the past twenty-two years for the Jell-O cream dessert. So here it is!

1 package Jell-O, any flavor (85 g)
1 cup boiling water (250 mL)
1 pint vanilla ice cream (500 mL)

Dissolve the Jell-O in the boiling water. Cut in the ice cream and stir until melted. Chill in the refrigerator — it doesn't really need more than 1 hour, but you can make it ahead of time. And it "sits" well.

Individual Cheesecakes

Serves 48

A perfect "finger" dessert.

2 8-ounce packages cream cheese (2 250 g)
1/2 cup sugar (125 mL)
1 teaspoon vanilla (5 mL)
3 eggs
1 box vanilla wafers
small paper baking cups
blueberry or cherry pie filling

Beat the cream cheese, sugar and vanilla together. Beat the eggs and add them gradually to the cheese mixture. Place a vanilla wafer in the bottom of each baking cup. Put these in small-sized muffin tins to prevent spreading. Add roughly 1 tablespoon (15 mL) of filling to each of these baking cups — not quite full. Bake in a 350°F (180°C) oven for about 15 minutes. Don't overcook as it tends to make them a bit dry.

Store in refrigerator for 2 to 3 days or freeze them. Just before serving, top with blueberry or cherry pie filling.

Note: I freeze these on cookie sheets then transfer them to a plastic bag for storing.

Chocolate Almond Roca Cheesecake

Serves 12 to 14

This recipe is slightly sensational.

Crust
1 cup chocolate wafer crumbs (250 mL)
1 cup ground almonds (250 mL)
1/3 cup melted butter (75 mL)

Combine all the ingredients and press into a 10 inch (3 L) tubeless, springform pan. Bake in a 350°F (180°C) oven for 10 minutes.

Filling
1 1/2 tablespoons gelatin (22 mL)
1/4 cup water (60 mL)
3 eggs, separated
1 1/2 cups sugar (375 mL)
1 cup warm milk (250 mL)
3 squares semisweet chocolate, melted
2 8-ounce packages cream cheese, at room temperature (2 250 g)
1/4 teaspoon almond extract (1 mL)
1/3 cup Amaretto liqueur (75 mL)
2 cups whipping cream (500 mL)
1 small can Almond Roca, crushed (in a blender)

Dissolve the gelatin in the water. Beat the egg *yolks* until light. Add 1 1/4 cups (310 g) of the sugar and the milk to the eggs. Cook this mixture in the top of a double boiler until thick. Remove from the heat and stir in the gelatin and melted chocolate. Cool for 5 minutes.

Beat the cream cheese with the almond extract and Amaretto. Combine well with the cooked chocolate custard. Cool over ice water until thick, stirring once while cooling. Beat the egg *whites* with the remaining sugar until stiff. Whip the cream. Fold the whipped cream into the egg whites and fold this into the chocolate-cheese mixture.

Pour the mixture into the springform pan *and* a 4 cup (1 L) mold. This recipe is sufficient for the springform pan plus the mold, which is nice to have for the family the next day because there will be no cheesecake left!

Chill well. Sprinkle the top with crushed Almond Roca before serving.

Orange Walnut Cheesecake   Serves 10 to 12

Cheesecakes probably rank number one as a party dessert. They freeze well and if it is to be a large party, it's fun to offer a variety—but how do you choose between Orange Walnut, Chocolate Almond Roca and Pumpkin-ginger Cheesecake with Pecan Crust?

Crust
1 cup vanilla wafer crumbs (250 mL)
1/2 cup finely chopped walnuts (125 mL)
1 teaspoon cinnamon (5 mL)
1/3 cup melted butter (75 mL)

Combine these ingredients and press them into the bottom of a 10 inch (3 L) tube cake, springform pan. Chill.

Filling
24 ounces cream cheese, room temperature (600 g)
3/4 cup sugar (175 mL)
3 large eggs
grated peel of 1 orange
3 tablespoons orange liqueur (45 mL)
1 1/2 tablespoons orange juice (22 mL)
1 1/2 teaspoons vanilla (7 mL)
4 tablespoons flour (60 mL)

Cream the cheese until smooth. Gradually add the sugar. Add the eggs one at a time. Add the orange peel, flavorings and flour. Pour this mixture into the springform pan and bake in a 350°F (180°C) oven for 30 to 35 minutes, until just firm. (If you use a springform pan, *tubeless* type, bake a little longer — 45 to 50 minutes.) Let sit for 20 minutes.

Topping
1 cup sour cream (250 mL)
1/4 cup icing sugar (60 mL)
1 teaspoon vanilla or orange liqueur (5 mL)
3/4 cup chopped walnuts (175 mL)

Combine the first 3 ingredients and spread this mixture on top of the cake. Return the cake to the oven for 5 minutes. Remove from the oven. Cool completely and sprinkle with walnuts and dust with icing sugar.

Pumpkin-ginger Cheesecake with Pecan Crust

Serves 10

Serve it and wait for the raves!

Crust
1 1/2 cups finely ground pecans (use a blender) (375 mL)
2 tablespoons sugar (30 mL)
1/4 cup melted butter (60 mL)

Combine all the ingredients and press the mixture into the bottom and 1/2 inch (1 cm) up the sides of a 10 inch (3 L) springform tube pan. You will need to flour your fingers a bit for this. Place some foil under the pan and up the edges slightly to catch any drips and bake in a 350°F (180°C) oven for 12 to 15 minutes.

Filling
2 8-ounce packages cream cheese, softened (2 250 g)
1 cup cereal cream (250 mL)
1 cup canned pumpkin (*not* pumpkin pie mix) (250 mL)
3/4 cup sugar (75 mL)
4 eggs, separated
1 teaspoon vanilla (5 mL)
1 teaspoon cinnamon (5 mL)
1/2 teaspoon ginger (2 mL)
1/2 teaspoon nutmeg (2 mL)
1/2 teaspoon salt (2 mL)
3 tablespoons flour (45 mL)

In the large bowl of a mixer combine the cream cheese, cereal cream, pumpkin, sugar, egg yolks and vanilla. Stir the spices and salt into the flour and add this to the first mixture. Beat the egg whites until stiff and fold in. Pour the mixture onto the crust and bake in a 325°F (160°C) oven for 50 to 60 minutes. Let cool for 20 minutes then pour on the topping.

Topping
1 cup sour cream (250 mL)
4 tablespoons sugar (60 mL)
1 tablespoon chopped, preserved ginger (comes in a jar) (15 mL)
1/2 teaspoon vanilla (2 mL)

Combine all the ingredients and pour over the cheesecake. Return the cake to the oven for an additional 5 minutes. Chill well before serving.

Note: This freezes well.

Daffodil Cake

Serves 10 to 12

A nice springtime dessert that invites you to make daffodils the theme of your party. Buy as many daffs as your budget will allow and have them all over the house — put a few in the center of your cake!

6 egg yolks
3/4 cup sugar (175 mL)
3/4 cup lemon juice (175 mL)
grated rind of 2 lemons
1/4 teaspoon salt (1 mL)
1 envelope unflavored gelatin
1/4 cup cold water (60 mL)
6 egg whites
3/4 cup sugar (175 mL)
1 large angel food cake
2 cups whipping cream (500 mL)
2 tablespoons icing sugar (30 mL)
1 teaspoon vanilla (5 mL)
12 lemon drops (garnish)

Mix the first 5 ingredients and cook in a double boiler until slightly thick. Remove from the heat. Soften the gelatin in the water and add it to the egg mixture. Set the mixture in the refrigerator to cool.

Beat the egg whites until stiff, gradually adding the sugar. Fold this into the cooled custard.

Shred the angel food cake with a fork and mix the pieces with the custard mixture. Pour this into a lightly greased angel food cake pan. Chill all day or overnight.

Whip the cream and add the icing sugar and vanilla. Unmold the cake and frost it with the whipped cream. Pound the lemon drops until they are almost powdered and garnish the cake with the candy.

Dieter's Delight
Serves 8

It's a very nice gesture to offer a choice of desserts for the benefit of friends who are trying to lose weight, one low-cal and one for those who are not dieting and look forward to that super-sweet at the end of the meal. When you have a dessert that does both—what a find! This is only 58 calories per serving.

2/3 cup orange juice (150 mL)
1 envelope unflavored gelatin
1/4 cup artificial sweetener (6 packets of Sugar Twin) (60 mL)
1 carton 2% cottage cheese (500 g)
1 small container of plain yogurt, 2% butterfat (200 g)
2 teaspoons vanilla (10 mL)
grated rind of 1 orange

Place the orange juice in small saucepan and sprinkle the gelatin over it to soften for about 5 minutes. Empty the artificial sweetener into the saucepan with the orange juice and gelatin and stir over very low heat, or very hot water, until the gelatin is dissolved. Let this cool to luke-warm. Place all the remaining ingredients in a blender or food processor and blend until smooth and creamy. With the motor still running, pour the orange juice mixture slowly into blender. Pour the mixture into a serving dish and let set in the refrigerator for a minimum of 4 hours.

Note: Unmold this dessert, spray a 4 to 6 cup (1 L to 1.5 L) mold with Pam or Mazola No-Stick before pouring the dessert into the mold.

Grand Marnier Pots de Crème
Serves 6

If you don't have any pots de crème (you may be tempted to buy some for this easy, elegant dessert), you may substitute any 4 to 5 ounce (125 mL to 150 mL) oven-proof containers, such as custard cups or individual soufflé dishes.

5 large egg yolks*
1/4 cup sugar (berry sugar is best) (60 mL)
1 1/2 cups whipping cream (375 mL)
3 1/2 tablespoons Grand Marnier (52 mL)
1/4 teaspoon vanilla (1 mL)

Beat the egg yolks and sugar together until thick and light colored. Turn the mixer to the lowest speed and gradually add the cream. Add the Grand Marnier and vanilla. Pour into 6 pots de crème. Place in a baking pan and pour enough water into the pan to cover the bottom 1 inch (2.5 cm) of the cups. Bake in a preheated 325°F (160°C) oven for 45 minutes or until a knife inserted in the middle comes out clean. Cool completely then place in the refrigerator to chill. Just before serving, place 1 teaspoon (5 mL) of topping over each serving.

Topping
2 teaspoons finely grated orange rind (10 mL)
1 1/2 tablespoons Grand Marnier (22 mL)

Combine these ingredients and use to decorate the tops of the dessert.

* You can save the whites to make the Meringue Cake on page 198; it freezes beautifully.

Marinated Fruit
Serves 2 to 4

Marinated fruit has to be one of the all-time easy summer desserts.

2 fresh peaches, peeled*, halved and pitted
　OR
1 pint fresh strawberries (225 g)
1 teaspoon sugar (5 mL)
1/2 to 3/4 cup Grand Marnier (125 mL to 175 mL)

Place the fruit in a jar. Sprinkle it with a little sugar (this is optional) and add the Grand Marnier. Do this in the morning or the day before.

Serve in large wine glasses — over ice cream or plain — and top with whipped cream.

Serves 2 if served plain, 4 if served with the ice cream.

* To peel peaches easily, immerse them in boiling water for 2 minutes.

Chocolate Crêpes
with Amaretto Sauce

Serves 8 to 10

The progress of feminism, which led women to the golf course, has not necessarily let them out of the kitchen. We still manage to produce some pretty great meals, they just have to be structured differently. This dessert is a perfect example. The crêpes can be made in the morning, the filling in the afternoon or the following day. Once the crêpes are filled, they are stored in the freezer until shortly before serving. Even the Amaretto Sauce can be made ahead and reheated, but it is so simple this is hardly necessary. (In a pinch, you could stir a little Amaretto into a commercial chocolate sauce.)

Crêpes
2 eggs
1/4 cup sugar (60 mL)
1/2 cup flour (125 mL)
2 tablespoons cocoa (30 mL)
1 cup milk (250 mL)
1 teaspoon vanilla (5 mL)
1 tablespoon melted butter (15 mL)

Combine all the ingredients in a blender and mix at *low* speed for 30 seconds. Let stand covered for 1 hour. Heat a crêpe pan over high heat and brush it with butter. Pour roughly 1/4 cup (60 mL) of batter in the pan and cook briefly on both sides. Stack with waxed paper separators. Makes 10 crêpes.

Filling
2 cups semi-sweet chocolate chips (500 mL)
1 1/2 teaspoons vanilla (7 mL)
pinch of salt
1 1/2 cups whipping cream, scalded (375 mL)
6 large egg yolks

Place the chocolate chips, vanilla and salt in a blender. Add the cream (the cream should be just below the boiling point for it has to be hot enough to melt the chocolate) and blend just until the chocolate is melted, about 20 seconds. Add the yolks and continue blending for about 5 seconds or until well blended. Cool (it will solidify when cold). When well chilled, place about 2 tablespoons (30 mL) of filling on each crêpe and roll. Place seam side down on cookie sheet and freeze. When well frozen, transfer the crêpes to a plastic container and keep frozen until shortly before you plan to serve them. Pass the following sauce.

Amaretto Sauce
6 ounce package semi-sweet chocolate chips (175 g)
1/4 cup cereal cream (60 mL)
3 tablespoons Amaretto liqueur (45 mL)
1/2 teaspoon vanilla (2 mL)

Melt the chocolate chips then stir in the remaining ingredients until well blended. Serve warm.

Flowerpot Dessert

Serves 8

A fun dessert, very easy to prepare and sure to delight your guests. These are really individual baked alaskas. The flowerpots are not expensive and can be used over and over. Adjust the flower in the pots to suit the occasion. Use sweetheart roses on Valentine's Day, holly for a Christmas party, daffodils for Easter, green carnations for St. Patrick's Day and for your golfing friends — a flag with 19 on it. Use a pipe cleaner and some green fabric. I will give approximate ingredients for 8 as that is my favorite number of guests to entertain.

8 small clay flowerpots
6 egg whites
1/2 cup sugar (preferably berry sugar) (125 mL)
1 plain cake
1 quart ice cream (1 L)
8 drinking straws

Sterilize the flowerpots ahead of time. (You can do this on sani-cycle in a dishwasher.) Make a meringue by beating the egg whites until soft peaks form, then beating in the sugar 1 tablespoon (15 mL) at a time. Place a piece of cake (I prefer pound cake) in the bottom of each flowerpot. It is important to cover the hole in the bottom of the pot. Spoon ice cream on top of the cake so that the pot is three-quarters full. Push a straw upright in the center of the ice cream. Fill the rest of the pot with meringue, leaving enough space over the opening of the drinking straw to insert a flower or decoration just before serving.

Bake in a 400°F (200°C) oven until the meringue is golden — 10 to 12 minutes. Serve immediately.

Note: These can be assembled ahead of time and kept in the freezer until ready to bake.

Deep-fried Ice Cream with Apricot Sauce

Serves 4 to 6

Not difficult at all — the name is deceiving. Make the ice cream balls ahead and keep them in the freezer until you're ready to fry. Make sauce ahead and reheat it at serving time. For more than 4 to 6, complete the dipping in batter and frying process a day or two ahead and freeze. Recrisp in hot oil just before bringing to table. This works very well.

Cream Puff Shells
1 cup water (250 mL)
1/2 cup butter (125 mL)
1/2 teaspoon salt (2 mL)
1 tablespoon sugar (15 mL)
1 cup sifted flour (250 mL)
4 eggs

Combine the water, butter, salt and sugar in a heavy saucepan and bring to boil. Add the flour all at once. Beat over low heat until the mixture leaves the sides of the pan and does not separate. Remove from the heat. Continue beating to cool the mixture a bit. Add the eggs one at a time. Beat until the mixture has a satiny sheen. Spoon onto buttered cookie sheet. Bake in a 375°F (190°C) oven for 40 to 50 minutes. Makes 12 to 14.

cream puff shells
vanilla ice cream
Apricot Sauce (page 53)

Cut the cream puffs in half and pull out as much of the soft inside as you can without creating any holes in the shells. Place a scoop of ice cream in one half and enclose it *completely* with the second half. Place the balls in the freezer. Just before serving, dip the frozen puffs in fritter batter and quickly deep-fry. Transfer to paper towels, then quickly to a serving plate.

Serve with Apricot Sauce or any sauce of your choice.

Fritter Batter

1 1/2 cups flour (375 mL)
2 tablespoons sugar (30 mL)
2 teaspoons baking powder (10 mL)
1/2 teaspoon salt (2 mL)
1 cup club soda (250 mL)
1 large egg, beaten

Make the batter by combining the dry ingredients then stirring in the club soda and egg. (When dipping, I find it best to use a poultry skewer — easy to penetrate and easy to slip off into hot fat.) Makes enough batter for 6 balls.

Chocolate Fondue   Serves 4

More and more young people are taking up golf — and young people love fondues!

6 tablespoons cereal cream (90 mL)
12 ounce package semisweet chocolate chips (350 g)
6 ounce package milk chocolate chips (175 g)
1/8 teaspoon salt (0.5 mL)
1 1/2 cups miniature marshmallows (375 mL)
1/2 cup sour cream (125 mL)
1 pound cake

Heat the cream but do *not* let it boil. Stir in the chocolate chips and salt until the chips start to melt. Add the marshmallows and stir until the marshmallows and chocolate are well combined and smooth. Remove from the heat and stir in the sour cream. Pour the chocolate sauce into a fondue pot (ceramic is best) and keep warm.

Cut the pound cake into bite sized pieces. Spear the cake with a fondue fork and dip it into the sauce.

Note: Marshmallows and fresh fruit make good dippers as well.

Meringue Cake
Serves 6

Two flat meringues with a banana-whipped cream filling between. You can make the meringues ahead — the rest is simple.

4 egg whites
1 cup berry sugar (250 mL)
1 teaspoon cornstarch (5 mL)
pinch of salt
1 teaspoon vinegar (5 mL)
1/2 teaspoon vanilla (2 mL)
powdered sugar

Beat the egg whites until almost stiff. Mix the sugar, cornstarch and salt and add them very gradually to the egg whites, beating well after each addition. Beat in the vinegar and vanilla a little at a time. Cut 2 8-inch (20 cm) square pieces of foil. Grease well and dust with powdered sugar. Put the foil on cookie sheets. Spread the meringue evenly over the pieces of foil. Bake in a 250°F (130°C) oven for 1 1/2 hours. Let cool, then carefully remove the foil.

Spread the following filling between the two layers and freeze for at least 3 hours. Remove from the freezer 1/2 hour before serving.

Filling
1 cup mashed bananas (250 mL)
2 teaspoons lemon juice (10 mL)
1/4 teaspoon salt (1 mL)
1 cup heavy cream (250 mL)
1/4 cup powdered sugar (60 mL)
1 teaspoon vanilla (5 mL)

Mash the banana with the lemon juice and salt. Whip the cream then add the powdered sugar and vanilla. Fold in the banana mixture.

Best-ever Chocolate Mousse
Serves 6

My daughter Lynn has a great sense of taste and is as enthusiastic about good food as I am. She arrived home from a restaurant one night and said she had had a marvelous chocolate dessert. I asked her to describe it and she answered, "It tasted like a cold melted-down chocolate bar with a hint of orange" — so we went to work. Here is the result.

6 ounce package chocolate chips (175 g)
2 eggs, room temperature
2 tablespoons icing sugar (30 mL)
3 tablespoons Grand Marnier (45 mL)
1 cup heavy cream, scalded (250 mL)
Grand Marnier (optional)

Place the first 4 ingredients in a blender. Add the cream (it should be scalded to the point of *almost* boiling). Blend until the mixture is smooth — about 60 seconds. Pour into 6 individual pots de crème or demi-tasse cups and chill well.

For an extra touch, float 1 teaspoon of Grand Marnier on top of each pot before serving. It is a real taste delight — dipping through the thin layer of orange liqueur into the creamy chocolate below!

Pineapple Coconut Squares   Serves 8 to 10

A great recipe for busy days. It sometimes takes me longer to decide what club to use approaching the green than it does to put this dessert together.

19 ounce can crushed pineapple, "in its own juice" (540 mL)
1 package white cake mix (super-moist)
1 cup *butter* (250 mL)
2/3 cup coarsely chopped walnuts (150 mL)
1 1/2 cups flaked coconut (375 mL)

Empty the *undrained* pineapple into the bottom of a 9 by 13 inch (3.5 L) oblong baking pan. Spread evenly. Sprinkle the cake mix on top. Slice the butter thinly and place it evenly on top of the cake mix. It cuts into 12 slices, which fits the pan very nicely. Sprinkle the nuts on top of the butter. Sprinkle the coconut on top of the nuts. Bake in a preheated 350°F (180°C) oven for 55 to 60 minutes.

Serve slightly warm with or without whipped cream. It's also good cold, but should be served the day it is baked.

Ginger Mousse

Serves 6 to 8

1 cup ginger marmalade (250 mL)
1 tablespoon lemon juice (15 mL)
1 teaspoon powdered ginger (5 mL)
1 package unflavored gelatin
1/2 cup cold water (125 mL)
2 cups whipping cream, whipped (500 mL)

Heat the marmalade and lemon juice in the top of a double boiler. Stir in the powdered ginger. Soak the gelatin in the cold water for 5 minutes then add it to the hot mixture. Stir until the gelatin is dissolved. When cool but not set, fold in the whipped cream. Pour into a very lightly oiled 4 cup (1 L) mold and chill for 4 hours or overnight.

Sherry Pudding

Serves 4

As easy as sinking a 2 inch putt!

20 large marshmallows
1 cup sherry (250 mL)
1 cup whipping cream (250 mL)
slivered almonds (garnish)

Melt the marshmallows in the sherry over hot water. Put this mixture in the refrigerator until it starts to gel — 2 hours or more. Beat the whipping cream and combine it with the marshmallow mixture. Beat together until smooth. Spoon into individual dishes and let set. Serve well chilled and garnished with slivered almonds.

Note: If you prefer a mocha flavor, substitute 1 cup (250 mL) strong hot coffee for the sherry and proceed as above. Garnish the coffee pudding with shaved chocolate.

Mary's Kiwi Sorbet

Serves 10 to 12

I have entered this in the dessert section but it was really designed as a palate cleanser, to be served between the salad course and the entrée. This is very "in" now at smart dinner parties. Mary has guarded this recipe up until now but has shared it with me because I am such a special friend *and* I traded her something for it!

1 cup sugar (250 mL)
2 cups water (500 mL)
6 ripe kiwi fruit, peeled and cut in chunks
2 tablespoons lemon juice (30 mL)
1/4 teaspoon salt (1 mL)
1/2 bottle champagne (optional)*

Dissolve the sugar in the water and bring it to a boil over medium heat. Boil for 5 minutes, stirring occasionally. Refrigerate this syrup until well chilled.

In a blender or food processor, blend the kiwi fruit with the lemon juice and salt until smooth. You need 2 cups purée for the amount of syrup—if you have a little less purée, just don't use all the syrup. Combine the syrup and purée and pour this mixture into an 8 inch (2 L) square pan, cover and freeze, stirring once every 1/2 hour until firm. This will take approximately 3 hours.

Early on the day of the party remove the sorbet from the freezer and let it sit at room temperature to soften slightly — about 15 minutes. Spoon 2 to 3 tablespoons (30 mL to 45 mL) into small glasses or ramekin dishes and pour a little champagne over the top of each. Place the dishes back in the freezer. Take out 10 minutes before serving (while the previous course is being served). Serve as a separate course just before the entrée.

Note: This can be made up to 3 weeks ahead.

* The champagne *is* optional, but it changes the sorbet from super to super-duper.

Joan's Frozen Soufflé with Hot Strawberry Sauce

Serves 4

I buy 1 dozen macaroons and eat 10 of them every time I make this dessert, so I only make it during the golfing season!

1 pint vanilla ice cream (500 mL)
2 macaroons, crumbled
4 teaspoons orange juice or Grand Marnier (20 mL)
1/2 cup heavy cream, whipped (125 mL)
1 1/2 tablespoons chopped toasted almonds (22 mL)
1 1/2 teaspoons powdered sugar (7 mL)

Soften the ice cream slightly. Stir in the macaroons, orange juice or Grand Marnier and whipped cream. Spoon into a 4 cup (1 L) mold and sprinkle the surface lightly with almonds and sugar. Cover with Saran and freeze until firm — overnight or at least 4 to 5 hours. Make the following sauce just before serving and pass it separately.

Hot Strawberry Sauce
1 pint fresh strawberries, cleaned and halved (225 g)
  OR
10 ounce package frozen sliced strawberries, thawed (275 g)
sugar to taste
4 teaspoons (20 mL) orange juice or Grand Marnier

Put the berries in a saucepan with the sugar and simmer until soft but not mushy. Remove from the heat and stir in the orange juice or Grand Marnier.

ULTRA EASY — DESSERTS

To peel citrus fruit, soak it in hot water for 5 minutes. All of the white membrane will come off with the peel.

A strand of spaghetti makes a great cake tester. It's longer than a toothpick and much more sanitary than a piece of straw plucked from your broom (or do people still do that?)!

For a "busy day" pie, turn drained cling peach halves face down in a baked pie shell. Sprinkle them with brown sugar then top with a combination of sour cream folded into an equal amount of whipped cream. Chill.

A spoonful of vodka over lemon sherbet makes a lovely "palate cleanser" at a gourmet dinner.

Keep a jar of applesauce in your refrigerator for this quickie dessert. "Plump" a few raisins in hot water for about 5 minutes. Add the raisins to the chilled applesauce along with a pinch of cinnamon. Pour the mixture into a shallow baking dish and cover it with brown sugar. Place the dish under the broiler until the sugar caramelizes (as in Creme Brulée). Or omit the raisins and put a layer of sour cream under the sugar. Delicious!

Overripe bananas on hand and no time to do any baking? Look up your favorite banana cake recipe and mash as many bananas as you need. Mix in a wee bit of lemon juice and freeze the mixture until your next baking day.

Use Pillsbury Buttermilk Biscuits for individual Strawberry Shortcakes.

To salvage one-year-old candied fruit, soak it in some sherry or orange juice.

Melted-down Mars Bars make the most fantastic sauce for ice cream!

For a lovely dessert, scoop out oranges, place the fruit in a blender with vanilla ice cream and a bit of Grand Marnier, blend, then refill the orange shells. Freeze then serve.

For two easy party pies, mix 1 liter each of Cool Whip and flavored yogurt (the largest containers sold are 1 liter). Pour the mixture into pie shells made with Dad's cookies instead of graham wafers. Freeze. Place the pies in the refrigerator 30 minutes before serving.

For a smashing summertime pie, fill a baked pie shell with fresh raspberries and glaze it with melted red currant jelly. Pass the whipped cream please!

For a slightly sensational dip for fresh fruit, especially strawberries, melt 125 g (about half a bag) of marshmallows and stir in some sour cream and a bit of Grand Marnier or Amaretto. Serve warm.

For a very quick Black Forest Cake, fold half a can of cherry pie filling into chocolate cake batter (from a mix!) and bake as usual. When the baked layers are cool, spread the remaining half can of pie filling between the layers. Frost with whipped cream and decorate with cherries. The cherries with the stems on are very impressive!

Have you ever thought of wrapping small, whole peeled bananas in thinly rolled pastry and baking them? Ten minutes in a 450°F (230°C) oven should do it. Roll the bananas in sugar and cinnamon before you wrap them in the pastry.

Here's a great Christmastime-anytime cookie! Melt 1 pound (450 g) of *white* chocolate in a 200°F (100°C) oven. Stir 1/2 cup (125 mL) of chunky peanut butter, 1 1/2 cups (375 mL) of miniature marshmallows, 1 cup (250 mL) of unsalted peanuts and 1 cup (250 mL) of Rice Krispies into the chocolate. Drop by small spoonfuls onto waxed paper to cool.

The Eighteenth Hole

SUGGESTED MENUS FOR 4 TO 6 PEOPLE

NUMBER 1
Mushroom Pâté, 15
Spinach Salad, 37
Well-dressed Ham Slice, 79
Baked Sweet Potatoes
Green Beans or Peas with Sautéed Fresh Mushrooms
Sherry Pudding, 200
Wine Semi-sweet white

NUMBER 2
Wild Rice and Mushroom Soup, 28
Shrimp and Chicken Breast in Tomato Sauce, 62
Spinach Noodles Sprinkled with Parmesan
Tossed Green Salad
Fresh Strawberries with Gilley Grand Marnier Sauce, 55
Wine Dry white

NUMBER 3
Oriental Dip with Fresh Vegetables, 11
Marinated Flank Steak, 71
Baked Potatoes or Rice
Broccoli Stir-fry, 113
Sliced Tomato Salad or
Tossed Green Salad with Quartered Tomatoes and Bean Sprouts
Sunshine Salad Dressing, 47
Baked Bananas with Grand Marnier Sauce, 185
Wine Red of any kind

NUMBER 4
Hasty Hots, 13
Joy's Cheese and Lettuce Salad, 34
Broiled Salmon Steaks with Sour Cream and Dill, 57
Parsleyed New Potatoes with Lemon Butter
Green Peas
Joan's Frozen Soufflé with Hot Strawberry Sauce, 208
Wine full-bodied white

NUMBER 5
Cream of Fiddlehead Soup, 25
Tossed Green Salad with Louise's Salad Dressing, 45, or
Marion's Yogurt Dressing, 47
Lemon-ginger Chicken Breasts, 94
Asparagus with Sour Cream Sauce, 111
White or Wild Rice
Best-ever Chocolate Mousse, 198
Wine full-bodied white

SUGGESTED MENUS FOR 8 PEOPLE

NUMBER 1
Fried Camembert, 4, or
Russian Blini, 2
Bombay Consommé with Cheese Balls, 23
Melba Toast,
Spinach Salad, 37
Mary's Kiwi Sorbet, 201
Individual Beef Wellingtons with Escargot Sauce, 74
French Peas, 120
Stuffed Tomatoes, 128, or
Carrots with Ginger-pecan Sauce, 114
Ginger Mousse, 200
Wine Dry sherry with the soup course; your best red with the meat course

NUMBER 2
Crab Wontons, 10
Patricia's Lemon Velvet Soup, 26
Greek Salad, 36
Roast Leg of Lamb with
Favorite Sauce for Lamb, 52
Crisp-crusted Potatoes, 126
Stuffed Eggplant, 118
Green Peas
Schnitz Pie, 180
Wine dry red

NUMBER 3
Lynn's Liptauer Cheese Spread, 6
Apricot Breast of Chicken, 90
Sweet Potato and Apricot Casserole, 126
Frenched Green Beans
Tossed Green Salad
Almond Cake Sorensen, 184
Wine full-bodied white

NUMBER 4
Liver Pâté, 14
Spinach, Leek and Potato Soup, 27
Smothered Shrimp, 68
Hot Fluffy Rice
Broiled Tomatoes, 129
Joyce's Meringue Pie, 177
Wine full-bodied white

NUMBER 5
Caviar Spread, 5
Wild Rice Casserole, 127
Rolled Roast Loin of Pork, 84
Crisp-crusted Potatoes, 126
Stuffed Acorn Squash, 129
Overnight Layered Salad, 38
Orange Walnut Cheesecake, 189
Wine Full-bodied white

SUGGESTED MENUS FOR 10 to 12 PEOPLE

NUMBER 1
Smoked Oyster Dip, 13
Jay's Chicken Breasts, 93
Long Grain and Wild Rice
Orange and Avocado Salad, 41
Chocolate Crêpes with Amaretto Sauce, 194
Wine Dry white

NUMBER 2
Lise's Crab and Cheese Spread, 7
Rolled Roast Loin of Pork, 84
Easy Potato Bake, 123
Broccoli Stir-fry, 113
Avocado Salad in Edible Bowls, 32
Barb Chapman's Mud Pie, 179
Wine dry red

NUMBER 3
Cheese Sticks, 17
Easy Baked Chicken, 90
Rice
Stuffed Tomatoes, 128
Tossed Green Salad
Chocolate Almond Roca Cheesecake, 188
Wine Dry or semi-sweet white

SUGGESTED MENUS FOR 20 to 25 PEOPLE

NUMBER 1
Crab, Shrimp, Lobster or Tuna Tarts, 8
Whole Baked Ham Studded with Cloves
Savory Broccoli Bake, 112
Carrots with Ginger-pecan Sauce, 114
Overnight Layered Salad, 38
Daffodil Cake, 191
Wine Semi-sweet white

NUMBER 2
Guacamole Party Dip, 12
Sweet and Sour Chicken, 100
Overnight Layered Salad, 38
Orange Walnut Cheesecake, 189
Wine Semi-sweet white

NUMBER 3
Mushroom Pâté, 15, or Beer Cheese, 6
Rolled Rib Roast of Beef
Onion Casserole, 119
Savory Broccoli Bake, 112
Frenched Green Beans with Sautéed Fresh Mushrooms
Sheila's Pumpkin Ice Cream Pie, 181
Wine Your best red

FAVORITE WINES

DRY WHITE
French Chablis
French Muscadet
California Fumé Blanc

MEDIUM WHITE
California Chenin Blanc
California Riesling
German
Italian Orvieto

FULL-BODIED WHITE
French White Burgundy
California Chardonnay
Alsace Riesling

DRY RED
French Bordeaux
French Médoc

LIGHT RED
French Beaujolais
Italian Valpolicella

FULL-BODIED RED
California Cabernet Sauvignon
French Châteauneuf-du-Pape
Spanish, e.g., Don Miguel Torres

INDEX